MUSIC ALONE

Books by Peter Kivy

Speaking of Art (1973)
*The Seventh Sense: A Study of Francis Hutcheson's Aesthetics
and Its Influence in Eighteenth-Century Britain* (1976)
The Corded Shell: Reflections on Musical Expression (1980)
Sound and Semblance: Reflections on Musical Representation
(1984)
*Osmin's Rage: Philosophical Reflections on Opera, Drama, and
Text* (1988)

MUSIC ALONE

Philosophical Reflections on the Purely Musical Experience

PETER KIVY

CORNELL UNIVERSITY PRESS

Ithaca and London

First published 1990 by Cornell University Press.
Second printing 1991.
First printing, Cornell Paperbacks, 1991.

International Standard Book Number 0-8014-2331-7 (cloth)
International Standard Book Number 0-8014-9960-7 (paper)
Library of Congress Catalog Card Number 89-35570
Printed in the United States of America

Librarians: Library of Congress cataloging information appears on the last page of the book.

To the memory of Paul Henle,
philosopher, teacher, critic;
my first guide in philosophy

4 different ways to responding to music

It will be generally admitted that Beethoven's Fifth Symphony is the most sublime noise that has ever penetrated into the ear of man. All sorts and conditions are satisfied by it. Whether you are like Mrs. Munt, and tap surreptitiously when the tunes come—of course, not so as to disturb the others—; or like Helen, who can see heroes and shipwrecks in the music's flood; or like Margaret, who can only see the music; or like Tibby, who is profoundly versed in counterpoint, and holds the full score open on his knee. . . .

responds just physically

E. M. Forster, *Howards End*

Contents

Preface

The title of this book is all that remains of two baroque and very Kantian alternatives. I once had thought to call it *Critique of Pure Music* but upon suitable reflection rejected that possibility because of the "transcendental" connotations such a moniker would have conveyed to anyone familiar with Kant's *Critiques*. For I mean to undertake no such imposing task as showing how "pure" music is possible—either all of it, or even some of it.

Kant, however, seemed to be stuck in my mind for some reason or other, and the second title, equally Kantian, that surfaced early on was *Music within the Limits of Music Alone*. That title seemed to me to capture, though somewhat wordily, what I was trying to do, which was to continue with a series of works on musical aesthetics, the first three of which, one way or another, dealt with the subject of "music *and* . . ."—music and representation, music and expression, music and drama—but the next of which was meant to address the most difficult subject of all: just plain music; music unaccompanied by text, title, subject, program, or plot; in other words, music alone.

Few philosophers have written about music at all, fewer still about pure instrumental music, sans everything. The reasons are not far to seek. Of the fine arts, music is, notoriously, the only one that requires a kind of technical knowledge and a conspicuously technical vocabulary in order to "speak with the learned." Hardly any but musicians ever acquire these things. Naturally enough, when musical problems have tempted philosophers, and other "humanists," they have been those, like the problem of opera, or expression, or representation, where extramusical incursions make it possible, even advisable, to do without the technical baggage. Furthermore, these are the problems the philosopher, for one, is peculiarly prepared to deal with, because they relate directly to the philosopher's special concerns: language, meaning, epistemology, perception, the philosophy of mind, and philosophical psychology—all of which give the philosopher if not proprietary rights to the above-mentioned musical problems, at least a vantage point unique to the discipline.

Only three "famous" philosophers in modern times have said anything about music alone that has been memorable or remembered. Leibniz coined a phrase that has fascinated many and been quoted often; but a phrase it remains and, as such, remains as unintelligible as the fragments of Heraclitus. Schopenhauer, on the other hand, said more, perhaps, than he should have; for what he did have to say contributed nothing, really, to our understanding of music alone. Of the three, only Kant made progress, and it is safe to say that the philosophy of pure music begins with him. This is one of those strange ironies in the history of ideas, for he was singularly unsuited to the task, both by lack of knowledge and by lack of musical inclination. (Schopenhauer at least played the flute.) But as Kant himself observed, genius is a law unto itself. It is altogether fitting, then, that the title of this book, if not much of its content, should pay some measure of homage to the sage of Königsberg.

But what has a philosopher to say about music alone that could not be said better, and with more authority, by those specially trained to the task: music historians, ethnologists, theorists, composers, performers? He or she has some credentials and some palpable subject matter, as I have said, when it comes to music *and.* . . . Where representation, expression, text, and drama are absent, however, what remains, surely, is solely the domain of the music professionals. Here is not the place to answer that question. What *this* philosopher has to say about music alone is said in the pages that follow, and *that* is the only and, it is to be hoped, sufficient answer he will give. It remains now to say merely that it is not for the philosopher to be, here or anywhere else, a "logic inspector." The music theorist and musicologist, where they are not doing philosophy themselves, do not require a philosopher to correct their errors. Their disciplines, like all responsible ones, are (or should be) self-regulating. But the philosopher can, perhaps, show in some general way how what the "professionals" do is relevant to musical perception and appreciation. And here I undertake a little of that sort of thing.

The book falls, quite naturally, into three parts. The first four chapters concern preliminaries: they delineate the subject and deal with some predecessors. Chapters 5, 6, and 7 contain the main argument, which concerns musical enjoyment, musical understanding, and their (so it is claimed) intimate relation. The eighth and ninth chapters broach the vexed question of music and the emotions, with the final chapter as a kind of coda to the whole.

Those other than philosophers have, of course, talked about the nature of musical appreciation and understanding. I hope it will be apparent to the reader as the book progresses that the way I talk about music is different enough to warrant a separate hearing—and enough the same to acquit me of the charge of *ignoratio elenchi.*

The opening pages of Chapter 6 are based for the most part on a brief article in the *Journal of Aesthetic Education.* Chapter 8 is a revised and somewhat expanded version of an essay in *What Is Music? An Introduction to the Philosophy of Music,* edited by Philip Alperson. And Chapter 9 appeared previously, in much the same form, in *Philosophic Exchange.* For permission to reprint, I am grateful, respectively, to Ralph Smith, editor of the *Journal of Aesthetic Education,* to Haven Publications, publisher of *What Is Music?,* and to Jack Glickman, editor of *Philosophic Exchange.*

I have benefited in this, as in my other books on philosophy and music, from the generous assistance of my colleagues in the profession. Donald Callen has read the complete manuscript and given me many useful comments. The same service has been performed by Douglas Dempster, to whom I owe a special debt not only for his philosophical but also for his musical expertise. And Kendall Walton, for the second time, has undertaken to read a manuscript of mine: his critical eye never ceases to amaze and to enlighten me. I am also grateful to Guy Sircello for critical comments on Chapter 9, which I have tried, at least, to answer in a parry but not, alas, in a thrust.

The entire manuscript has been superbly edited by Roger Haydon, who has the rare gift of being able to improve an author's style without changing it. An author can ask no more.

Finally, I want to thank Ian Milligan for reminding me of the passage from E. M. Forster's *Howards End,* which serves not merely as the epigraph of this book but, indeed, as its theme. I hope the reader therefore will study the epigraph with more than just casual attention. It is not an ornament. It is the beginning of the argument. Tibby, Helen, Margaret, and Mrs. Munt are the guides.

Here, as elsewhere, I have been extremely fortunate in the help I have been given by those, most of whom I now count not only as fellow workers in the field but as friends as well. The errors that remain in this book are due not to them, or to my lack of respect for their opinions—which could not be higher—but to a strain of stubbornness in me that no amount of good advice is able to dislodge and yet is, at the same time, I suppose, essential for the enterprise.

PETER KIVY

New York City

MUSIC ALONE

CHAPTER I /

Why Music?

In the *Essai sur l'origine des langues* (1764), Jean-Jacques Rousseau reports on an eighteenth-century curiosity that has, from time to time, fascinated musicians and inventors. "I have seen," he writes, "that famous keyboard on which they claim to make music with colours."[1] He doesn't think much of the claim, and neither, for different reasons, do I.

Why should there not be "music of colours," though, or, more generally, a "visual music"? And if the answer is, There should be, then, one naturally feels impelled to respond: Why hasn't there been?

Perhaps there hasn't been a visual music because we have never had an adequate technology for producing it. Whatever clumsy machinery was available in Rousseau's time, involving candles or lamps, could not possibly have resulted in anything approaching the complexity—both vertical and horizontal—that could be produced by the harpsichord, organ, or orchestra (small though each one may have been by modern standards). And although there is no way of totally refuting this claim about technology, somehow our intuitions (or at least my intuitions) point in another direction.

1. Peter le Huray and James Day, eds., *Music and Aesthetics in the Eighteenth and Early-Nineteenth Centuries* (Cambridge, 1981), p. 100.

I

Now, as a matter of fact, we do have a quite impressive array of technical equipment and techniques for producing visual music. We have had them ever since the invention of the moving-picture camera and projector; animation techniques, as well as videographics, have expanded the possibilities still further. There is, indeed, a considerable history of experimentation, in the twentieth century, with totally abstract, nonrepresentational sequences of patterns and colors that can fairly be described as "music for the eyes." Nor can it fairly be denied that some of these experiments have led to artistic success, at least in some *small* way.

But I underscore "small" to suggest that visual music has been unable to sustain itself to any significant length, at least in terms of the tolerance of a normal viewer (not the fanatic) for such things. A person of no particular musical expertise, with only limited musical enthusiasms, can listen, with more or less rapt attention, to a concert of chamber music that may last for two hours. Nothing even approaching this attention span seems possible for visual music. Why is this?

The only answer I can venture, which amounts to the purest speculation, is an evolutionary one. Certainly Rousseau seems to be correct in asserting that to try to make visual music "is to put the eye in place of the ear and the ear in place of the eye."[2] But what *are* their places? Certainly, from the standpoint of natural selection, the place of the eye is as the "survival" sense par excellence. "Primates," says Stephen Jay Gould, "are visual animals."[3] Indeed, they may, from the evolutionary biologist's point of view, be definitionally so. For, we are told by an expert in this area, "recent neurophysiological and neuroanatomical data suggest that at least one unique defining feature for the order Primates does exist. In all mammals the retina projects to the optic tectum, but the manner in which the visual field is represented in the optic tectum of Primates

2. Ibid.
3. Stephen Jay Gould, *Time's Arrow, Time's Cycle: Myth and Metaphor in the Discovery of Geological Time* (Cambridge, Mass., 1987), p. 18.

differs from that found in all other mammals."[4] And without
following this discussion into its inevitable and, for our purposes here, unnecessarily technical detail, the special manner in
which the visual field is represented in the optic tectum of
Primates adds up to a biologically and evolutionarily superior
organ.

The survival value of vision is obvious enough. As Le Gros
Clark observes, "the visual sense is the most informative of
the discriminative senses, for it provides a means whereby
objects may·be recognized near at hand or in the far distance in
regard to their position, form, texture and colour, and enables
spatial properties to be defined with an accuracy which is hardly approached by the use of other sensory mechanisms." It is
no surprise, therefore, given the evolutionary advantage that
vision so obviously bestows and the equally obvious evolutionary success of the Primates, particularly *homo sapiens,* that,
as Clark continues, "all the modern Primates are characterized
by a high degree of elaboration of the visual centres of the
brain . . . and . . . the increasing dominance of the visual
sense played a significant part in the evolution of the group as a
whole." Equally unsurprising is that the sense of hearing declined as a survival sense for Primates. Even the crudest ana-
tomical evidence verifies this notion, Clark makes apparent:
"It might be supposed from the circumstance that in the higher Primates the external ear is relatively small and appears to
have undergone retrogressive changes, that this indicates a
lesser degree of auditory acuity than that possessed by lower
mammals with large mobile ears. To a certain extent this is no
doubt true."[5] And although, Clark points out, the correlation
of size and mobility of the external ear with auditory acuity is
not infallible—the external ear surfaces also serving as a tem-

4. John Altman, "Reconstructing the Evolution of the Brain in Primates
through the Use of Comparative Neurophysiological and Neuroanatomical
Data," *Primate Brain Evolution: Methods and Concepts,* ed. Este Armstrong and
Dean Falk (New York, 1982), p. 13.

5. W. E. Le Gros Clark, *The Antecedents of Man: An Introduction to the
Evolution of the Primates* (Chicago, 1960), pp. 266, 273, 281.

perature regulator in some animals—it is sufficient here, I think, as prima facie evidence for the claim that as, in the modern Primates, including man, the sense of sight has advanced in acuity and (therefore) in survival value, so the sense of hearing has concomitantly declined in both departments.

It remains now, to complete my conjecture, only to suggest that because we have evolved with the sense of sight paramount in our survival, we have evolved "hard-wired," to a certain extent, to see "defensively"; which is to say, we are compelled to place "realistic" or "representational" interpretations on visual perceptions. It is a knee-jerk reaction to protect us from potential danger, a phenomenon well known to psychologists through various experiments and, of course, well illustrated in the interpretation of the Rorschach blots. But if that is the case, then we are at cross-purposes when we are presented with the visual analogue of music alone. For what we are meant to do with "visual music," as with pure instrumental music, is to perceive abstract, nonrepresentational, frequently expressive patterns, forms, and perceptual qualities, and enjoy them *qua* abstract and expressive patterns, forms, and qualities. And if our whole visual apparatus is geared to do just the opposite thing—to place realistic, representational interpretations on what we see—we will have little and laborious success in perceiving and enjoying visual music. We may sustain the attitude of noninterpretive vision, but only for short periods of time—which is precisely why visual music has amounted to compositions that are very brief compared even to the moderate length of a Haydn string quartet.

And it is no good to say that what the visual musician will do, then, is to compose visual forms that utterly defeat our "seeing as" propensity. For this propensity cannot be defeated: evolution has seen to that. There appears to be no form so representationally barren that we cannot and do not see it as something or other, sooner or later. That is why we see things in clouds and ink blots.

But at least in the human species, and it is human music of

which I speak, the ear does not play that survival role—and for good reason, given the survival advantages of light over sound as the bearer of danger signals. Thus the ear, far more than the eye, is capable of sustained perceiving in an abstract, noninterpretive mode. It is not to the same degree hard-wired to interpret. And that, I suggest, is why there is not, and is unlikely ever to be, a visual analogue of a Beethoven string quartet or a Bruckner symphony.

Here, however, it may well be objected that the argument, such as it is, is likely to prove too much rather than too little. For if the sense of hearing plays less of a role than the eye in our survival, the olfactory sense, the sense of taste, and the sense of touch have lower survival profiles than even audition does. So the conclusion seems to be that we ought to have symphonies of smells, tastes, and "feels" far more elaborate than the paltry symphonies of sound that even the most long-winded practitioners of that art have given us. And such, needless to say, is clearly not the case.

Here one must introduce a second variable. What we must have, I suppose, to sustain the kind of interest in pure perception that music alone represents, is *both* a survival profile low enough to defeat interpretational perceiving for substantial periods of time *and* an acuity, a complexity, a delicacy of the sense organ enabling it to take in objects of a sufficiently complex and interesting magnitude: that is, objects complex enough and interesting enough to occupy us significantly.

There may perhaps be other arguments against a "music" of touch, taste, and smell, arguments based on ruling out the objects of these senses, on conceptual grounds, as possible aesthetic or artistic objects.[6] For my own part, I see no theoretical objection to the possibility of minimal compositions that might aptly be described as "music" for touch, taste, or

6. Roger Scruton, for example, presents an argument against foods and taste being "aesthetic" in his *The Aesthetics of Architecture* (Princeton, N.J., 1980), pp. 71–74. For a reply to his argument, see Barbara Savedoff, "Intellectual and Sensuous Pleasure," *Journal of Aesthetics and Art Criticism* 43 (1985).

smell. As for visual "music," it is not merely a possibility but a going concern, if a minor one. I am persuaded, rather, that we have an elaborate art of sound music, rather than touch, taste, or smell music, for purely empirical reasons, although this state of affairs may be empirically "necessary" for any intelligent species like our own capable of music, due to the physical nature of light, sound, and living matter. It is the peculiar nature of our evolutionary history as a species that we have the sense of hearing developed to just that level of complexity, acuity, and delicacy, and just that role in our biological lives, enabling it to perceive much but not too much.

In contrasting the senses of sight and hearing, however, it is important to note that the latter is not entirely without its own tendency to "interpret"—to "hear as." Indeed, as I have argued elsewhere, it is because of our strong tendency to hear music as "animate," as (at times) emotive utterance, that we perceive emotive properties in music; hear music expressively.[7] Nevertheless, there is not in hearing, as there is in sight, that almost overpowering propensity to put a pictorial interpretation on even the most abstract or "formless" congeries of lines and patterns. This is my experience, and I ask the reader if it is not hers or his as well. One cannot seem to help "seeing things" in visual patterns. If the compulsion can be quelled at all, it is only with great effort, for very brief periods. Hearing places no such pictorial burden on us; not only do we not tend to hear "pictorially," we have great difficulty in doing so at all, as the relative poverty of musical representation abundantly attests.[8]

To my claim that vision is the preeminently interpretive sense because of its paramount survival status in man, and hearing far more relaxed in that regard (even degenerate, as the evolutionists might put it), it could be replied that I have

7. Peter Kivy, *The Corded Shell: Reflections on Musical Expression* (Princeton, N.J., 1980), especially pp. 57–59.

8. On the limits and possibilities of representation in music, see Peter Kivy, *Sound and Semblance: Reflections on Musical Representation* (Princeton, N.J., 1984).

overlooked the all-important linguistic function of the aural faculty. For surely, so the objection would go, if the eye is predisposed to read visual stimuli realistically or representationally rather than abstractly, the ear is predisposed, at least since the advent of language, to interpret aural stimuli as meaningful linguistic utterance rather than as meaningless noise. So whereas "visual music" would, indeed, be defeated by the eye's propensity to interpret visual stimuli as objects (or their representations) in the world, pure "music," properly so called, would be defeated by the ear's linguistic propensity to interpret aural stimuli as sentences in the language of the listener. Thus the eye and the ear are on all fours with one another with regard to the "instinct" for interpreting, although they are prone to interpret for different results; and so it cannot be adduced as an explanation for why there is *music* but not "visual music" that the former appeals to a noninterpretive sense, permitting of purely contentless perception.

The answer to this objection must be, I think, that far more information is required to make sounds linguistically meaningful than to make visual stimuli interpretable as objects in the world. In listening to indistinct speech, we doubtless fill in many of the missing sounds, as well as filter out the noise, to "construct" an intelligible message; what we expect has a great deal to do with what we "hear." This is well-known; were it not so, communication through speech would not be possible. But all of this cannot add up to anything remotely like an equality of interpretive success.

It seems nearly impossible to defeat the interpretive capacity of the eye given stimuli that can be constituted as perceived form. Only a completely uniform expanse—the blackness of impenetrable darkness, for instance, or an unbroken vista of blue sky—will perhaps do the business. But where visual form is discernible, interpretation can and inevitably does seem to take place. In other words, "seeing as" or "seeing in" seems undefeatable. But surely the same cannot be said for putting a meaningful construction on sounds, for the parameters of meaning are far too stringent to allow for the same freedom of interpretation. If short-wave static is the aural analogy of clouds, it hardly wants arguing that hearing intelligible language in the former does not take place, whereas seeing objects in the latter seldom fails.

One interesting sidelight of this comparison between the eye and the ear is the frequency with which theorists try to make pure music out to be meaningful as opposed to representational. How frequently since the advent of pure instumental music in the West, have we heard such claims as the following: "[a] piece of music is a communication. And if you are one of those to whom a Beethoven symphony is a lot of meaningless noise, you may say: 'Tell me what it communicates'—meaning, of course, 'Tell me in words.' But the simple inescapable fact of the situation is that what Beethoven says in those sounds cannot be told in words."[9] What all such claims essentially amount to is the expression of a very strong feeling or impression that musical sounds are meaningful, accompanied by an inevitable recognition that they really are not (the latter signaled by inability to state what their meaning is), decked out as a profundity about their meaning being "nonverbal," or "special," or "too precise for mere discursive language to express."

Such perennial attempts to give music meaning suggest we are perfectly right in suspecting a tendency of the ear to interpret sound linguistically when given the least opportunity. And music does, indeed, offer that opportunity. For unlike random noise or even ordered, periodic sound, music is quasi-syntactical; and where we have something like syntax, of course, we have one of the necessary properties of language. That is why music so often gives the strong impression of being meaningful. But in the long run syntax without semantics must completely defeat linguistic interpretation. And al-

9. B. H. Haggin, *The Listener's Musical Companion,* 2d ed. (New York, 1959), p. 4.

though musical meaning may exist as a theory, it does not exist as a reality of listening.

A second sidelight, already alluded to, can be stated very briefly. If the tendency of the ear to interpret musical sound as meaningful human utterance fails, as it must, what *linguistically* is left? Take the meaning away from the utterance, and one thing you *may* still have (though not necessarily) is the utterance's emotional cast. I can, for example, sometimes tell by tone of voice that someone has said something to me angrily or sadly, even though *what* he or she said may have been lost on the wind. And the musical equivalent of the emotional tone of voice is, I have argued elsewhere, and others have argued before me, a prime mover in the recognition of what emotions music is expressive of. Thus the tendency of the ear to hear sound linguistically lends support to the claim that part of music's expressive quality is due to the analogy of musical sound to passionate human speech. For although the tendency of the ear to hear music linguistically is easily defeated on the semantic level, as we have seen, it may not be so easily defeated at another linguistic level, that of emotional significance, where semantic parameters are not always required. And the evidence bears this suggestion out in the twin observations that we can never say what pure instrumental music means (in the semantic sense of that word) but frequently can, within certain limits, say what it is expressive of.

The conclusion of these observations, then, is that although the ear does, like the eye, have a strong tendency to interpret, its tendency is not to interpret sounds as representational or as natural phenomena but to interpret them as meaningful in the full linguistic sense. And since such a tendency is easily defeated by the stringent semantic requirements on successful linguistic interpretation, it puts up no impediment to the appreciation of pure, abstract musical sound while it contributes to the perception of expressive properties. This is not to say, of course, that the ear does not also tend to interpret sound naturalistically. But that tendency, I have argued, has weakened

[handwritten margin note: There's meaning here but def 't]

through natural selection, both in man and in other Primates, even as the visual sense has developed to the ascendancy it now enjoys. Thus where the ear tends to hear realistically, the tendency is weak, and its weakness defeats it in the face of pure musical structure. And where it tends to hear linguistically, though that tendency is strong, the stringent requirements of successful semantic interpretation more than compensate for its strength and defeat easily, in a structure with syntax but no semantics, both the successful outcome and, indeed, the attempt itself. Such, at any rate, is my hypothesis.

Here, then, is our situation. Visual music and the (perhaps merely possible) music of taste, touch, and smell are limiting cases, with the music of sound (real music, if you will) sandwiched in between. At the top of the sandwich we have "music for the eyes." Sight, of course, provides possibilities of perceptual complexity and fineness of discrimination that far exceed even those of hearing and certainly those of taste, touch, and smell. That there is no sophisticated tradition of visual music, as there is of the aural kind, requires some explanation other than the paucity of sense discrimination. The explanation I venture, not at all confidently but as perhaps nothing more than a flight of fancy, is that music alone requires a kind of noninterpretive perception unavailable, for evolutionary reasons, to the sense of sight. We can, in vision, sustain short periods of pure, "phenomenological" perception, often, I think, at considerable cost in psychological effort, thus making possible the minor art of visual music and, of course, the more substantial and entrenched traditions of decoration and nonrepresentational painting and sculpture.

These more or less well-established modes of objectless painting, sculpture, and design, by the way, should not be viewed as counterexamples to the explanation here offered for the severe limitations of visual music. For the way we must attend to music, it being a temporal art, is very different from the way we attend to, say, a painting by Jackson Pollock. A late Haydn string quartet, which at fifteen to twenty minutes places very moderate demands on our temporal patience, far exceeds the unbroken temporal demands made upon us by a nonobjective painting. That is not because the painting will not reward twenty minutes of our attention whereas the Haydn string quartet will, but because the music demands twenty consecutive minutes of our time, where the Jackson Pollock does not and seldom gets it. We (I) look at a painting for three or perhaps five minutes, glance away, come back to it, concentrate on a region, break attention again—*sustained* perception comes in short, interrupted spurts. Were we, however, to attend this way to a musical composition, we would fail completely to take it in. One cannot, of course, "glance away" from a Haydn string quartet and then return to find it waiting: the musical events have passed by. It would be like looking at a painting with holes cut out of it.

To return to our musical sandwich: at the bottom are the "musics" of touch, taste, and smell. They cannot get off the ground, not because the appropriate senses cannot be employed "phenomenologically" to attend to the pure qualities of their objects but because their rather limited capabilities, compared to hearing and sight, make substantial "compositions" for them, on the scale of musical sound structures, impossible. Whatever might be accomplished along these lines would be severely limited, although the appreciation of fine wine and food does seem to me to embody a kind of experience that might be described as "aesthetic"—but not, I think, as "musical." Lying low on the survival scale (I take it no one will confuse the survival value of *eating* with that of *tasting*), the three "lower" senses do achieve that noninterpretational stance required for music alone. But even in the master chef and sommelier, they do not possess the fineness and complexity of discrimination that can sustain a tradition approaching in kind or degree the tradition of instrumental music in the West.

But there, in the middle of the sandwich, is wonderful, glorious sound, the gift of an indulgent natural selection that gave our ears enough of the action to make them the fine instruments they are but not enough to make them, like the eyes, the slave of duty. And so we have that "most sublime noise" in which Margaret can only see music—a compliment from me but not from her creator.

Well, what of all this? Let me say straightaway that the arguments and philosophical positions in this book in no way depend upon these wild speculations being truth or even close to it. Where my arguments and positions begin is with the existence of music alone as a fait accompli, whatever brought it into being or made it possible. Perhaps the question Why music? is one of those senseless questions people put without having any clear idea about what a satisfactory answer could possibly be. Why put it, then? What I want to do, in putting it, is to convey some of my sense of wonder at the whole phenomenon of music alone; and that sense of wonder begins with what seems to me to be the genuine, if insoluble, mystery of why we have "pure" music at all, and why, since we do, we don't have "music" for our other sense modalities. The color organ is a curiosity; Bach's organ fugues are a monument to the human spirit. This is where my wonder begins, the analogue, if you will, of the metaphysicians's wonder at why there is something rather than nothing. Maybe the only answer to my question is the same as that famous answer to the metaphysician's: Why *not?*

But, of course, my "metaphysical" wonder does not end with the question of why there is musical something rather than nothing. For it also seems wonderful to me, and mysterious, that people sit for protracted periods of time doing nothing but listening to meaningless—yes, *meaningless*—strings of sounds. What is going on here? What *are* these people doing? What's in it for them? We *do* have music alone and have had, as I construe it, as a going concern, in the West since at least the end of the sixteenth century. What is the nature of our involvement and fascination with it? These questions I shall try to answer in what follows. But I am bound to say that

where does Fantasia fit in

when I finish, I will still, I think, retain that sense of wonder and mystery about the whole enterprise. My answers seem to me shallow next to the profundity of what I am talking about: the *Well-Tempered Clavier* or the C♯-Minor String Quartet. How *can* there be a philosophy of *that?*

CHAPTER 2 /

What Music?

The kind of music I am concerned with in this book began to be written sometime toward the close of the sixteenth century. This is a very vague generalization to make, and I will try to clean it up a bit before I proceed. But before I do, I want to emphasize that it doesn't really matter much. I could, philosophically, go straight to the heart of the matter by simply saying that the kind of music I am concerned about is the kind of which Bach's *Well-Tempered Clavier* and Beethoven's C♯-Minor String Quartet are paradigm cases, and let the reader decide what other things are of that kind: Indian ragas, gamelan music, instrumental dances of the Middle Ages and Renaissance, Dixieland, what you will. I don't choose to take the easy way of definition by example yet, however, because I want to give just a little thought to the outlines and vagaries of the "kind" in question.

It is not entirely arbitrary—but let us, for the sake of argument, assume it is—to choose (say) the *canzoni per sonar* of Giovanni Gabrieli or the English viol fantasias, music like that, as something like the beginning of the pure, instrumental music tradition in the West. I know music was played on instruments alone before that time, and some of it was written with an instrumental performance specifically in mind. But music for instruments is not merely a tradition, it is something like an institution, or complex of institutions, marking out *a way of responding;* and that, it seems to me, we begin to get, along with other modern institutions, ways of life, and modes of thought, at the start of the seventeenth century. That this music now has a place in the modern repertoire doesn't prove anything, of course, about the intentions of its creators. After all, we hang African masks in museums of art. However, it does say a lot about what is "in" this music that modern brass ensembles, for example, treat Gabrieli's pieces in much the same way modern string quartets treat the classical string quartet: as the core around which they define their enterprise.

Now just because it is customary to play things on instruments rather than sing them, and just because they have no accompanying text, title, program, or other literal hint that they are not to be taken as pure musical structure, it does not follow that these things are "pure music," what I have been and will be calling "music alone." Or at least it does not follow that they are *only* music alone. The canzoni of Gabrieli were, after all, ceremonial pieces, not meant for the Carnegie Recital Hall. Handel's organ concertos were "fillers" at the oratorios. Mozart's wind band divertimenti were functional compositions for social occasions. His and Haydn's unnumbered minuets were meant to be danced to and only secondarily, one supposes, listened to. And a great deal of Bach's best-known keyboard music had a quasi-didactic intent.

How, then, shall we "define" music alone? If we are wise, we will not try to define it at all; for our attempts, doubtless, will exclude either too much or too little and raise other philosophical problems as well. If we say that music alone is music intended by the composer to be responded to in a certain way, for example, the way Margaret and Tibby but *not* Helen responded to Beethoven's Fifth, we will be ruling out just those kinds of music—Gabrieli's canzoni, Mozart's wind divertimenti, a lot of Bach's keyboard music—where the composer's intent was "mixed." We can, perhaps, patch things up a bit by

[margin annotation: Prefer's to give concrete examples classical tradition]

saying something like: Music alone is music composed with *one* of the leading intentions being that it be responded to in such and such a way. This definition is something of an improvement, as it would include compositions that might not have one appropriate and overarching compositional intent. However, there would remain in the patched-up intentional definition, as in the more simplistic one, the additional problem of determining *what* the composer's intention or intentions might have been, and what we would make of it or them, anyway, if we didn't find what we were looking for.

To begin with, for almost any piece of instrumental music (or any other music, for that matter), we do not have any independent knowledge of the composer's intentions in composing it; independent, that is, of the music itself and the traditions and institutions in which it exists. Our best—and usually our only—evidence for Haydn's having intended his mature string quartets and symphonies to be music alone is that they will sustain such a hearing, richly and satisfactorily, and that they were produced in a network of appropriate institutions and practices. But from the intentionalist's point of view, that puts the cart before the horse. (From my point of view, it gets things exactly right most of the time.) For far from knowing Haydn's mature quartets and symphonies are music alone by knowing that Haydn intended them to be responded to in that way, we infer (if we care to) that Haydn intended them to be responded to as music alone from their being eminently susceptible of such a response and existing in a social context and practice in which such a response is invited. Thus we cannot be defining music alone as music intended to be responded to in that way (whatever that way is), since first we must know, in most instances, that it is music alone before we determine that that is how it was intended.

Second, even in the rare cases in which we do have adequate evidence of intention, external to the work or the institutions in which it was composed and performed, it does not seem at all clear that expression of intention will of itself be decisive. It would be instructive, in understanding this point, if we could test our intuitions against two kinds of case: a case of authorial intention seeming to go against our perception that the work *is* music alone, pure music, and a case of authorial intention seeming to go against our perception that it is *not*. Fortunately, two specific cases do come to my mind.

Arthur Honegger's *Pacific 231* seems a paradigm, if ever there was one, of "representational" music. It has a title, and, for those who are not railroad buffs, the composer tells us, in the introductory remarks to the Salabert edition of the full score, just what that tile refers to: "The subject of my composition was an engine of the 'Pacific' type number 231 used for heavy loads and built for great speed." Anyone who has lived in the age of steam immediately recognizes, sometimes even without knowing the title of the piece, the uncanny skill with which Honegger has represented the sound of a railway steam engine at rest, accelerating, at speed, decelerating, and at rest again. Yet in the remarks to which I have already alluded, the composer also says this extraordinary thing: "In 'Pacific 231' I have not aimed to imitate the noise of an engine."

Now, the resemblance of the musical sounds to those of a railway steam engine is too close for us to be able *not* to hear it, if we were of a mind to take Honegger's explicit statement not to have intended this resemblance as an absolute injunction not to treat the work, even in part, as a representation of railway noises. Of course, the inability to refrain from hearing a piece of music in a certain way is itself not decisive. Unfortunately, because of a childhood devoted to the radio, I cannot help but hear one passage in *Fidelio,* and another in Gluck's *Orfeo,* as phrases from advertising jingles of the 1940s; but the ineradicable propensity in me and others in my generation to hear these things in those works hardly makes the works, *per impossibile,* representations of the jingles. However, if we put together Honegger's title with the absolutely undeniable resemblance of the musical sounds of *Pacific 231* to the sounds of a railway steam engine, and place the work in the political and

aesthetic contexts of the times in which it was composed, then
we have a choice. We can take his expression of intention at
face value and conclude that the resemblance is purely acciden-
tal, therefore aesthetically irrelevant, not a part of the work,
which certainly flirts with the impossible; or we can override
his expressed intention to *not* represent, either by ignoring it or
by reinterpreting it (which amounts, really, to the same
thing).

  If we simply say that Honegger's intention to represent is
not necessary for *Pacific 231*'s being, as it appears to be, a
representation of the sounds of a steam engine, we are beset
with a well-known cluster of philosophical problems, including the insuperable one (it seems to me) of having to have
unintended representations. Those who wish to avoid them
might reinterpret what Honegger seems to be saying as a form
of hyperbole. The judicious addition of a "merely" and an
"also" in the appropriate places yields Honegger's complete
thought as: "In 'Pacific 231' I have not [*merely*] aimed to imitate the noise of an engine, but [*also*] rather to express in terms
of music a visual impression and physical enjoyment." This
operation, of course, avoids the oddity, bordering on logical
absurdity, of unintended representations. But this approach
too has its philosophical danger, as it appears to make the
conflict between the intention not to represent and the representationality of the work impossible by stipulation: by fiat.
That is to say, one simply refuses to consider *anything,* no
matter how obviously it expresses the intention not to represent, as an expression of that intention, if the work belies it
strongly enough.

  My purpose here is not to plump for one alternative or the
other, although it seems plain to me that representation without intention is conceptually impossible.[1] All I wish to suggest, for present purposes, is that it does appear that, from the

  1. On this see Peter Kivy, *Sound and Semblance: Reflections on Musical Representation* (Princeton, N.J., 1984), pp. 212–215, and Kivy, *The Corded Shell:
Reflections on Musical Expression* (Princeton, N.J., 1980), pp. 64–66.

point of view of the sophisticated musical listener untainted by philosophical theory, the composer's *apparent* intention not to represent will not be decisive against strong enough indications to the contrary in the work—title, for example, and surrounding institutional practices, combined with a powerful impression of representationality. Those without my logical scruples may simply say "intentions be damned." Those who share them will be compelled to reinterpret the rare cases where external expressions of intention are available to suit their conceptual requirements. But in either case the musical experience will be decisive, and external expressions of intention, no matter how convincing, unavailable as material for a definition of music alone, at least in the form of necessary or sufficient condition.

What of the complementary case, the case of an expressed intention to represent and a work that does not bear any clear indications, either in its musical content or in the context in which it presents itself, of anything but pure instrumental music? We have an example that at least suggests this possibility, in the magnificent slow movement, *adagio affetuoso ed appassionato,* of Beethoven's String Quartet in F, Op. 18, No. 1. According to Beethoven's friend Karl Amenda, the composer wrote this movement with the vault scene of *Romeo and Juliet* in mind; and Gustav Nottebohm, the reigning nineteenth-century expert on Beethoven's sketches, "was able to read '*les derniers soupirs*' over an early sketch for the end of the movement."[2]

One might, if so inclined, take these anecdotal scraps as external evidence—that is, evidence external to the work—of Beethoven's intention that the second movement of Op. 18, No. 1, be heard as a musical representation of the death of the two star-crossed lovers: or, in other words, of intention that it be not a piece of pure instrumental music, music alone, but a musical representation of fictional events.

2. Joseph Kerman, *The Beethoven Quartets* (New York, 1967), p. 36.

Should this expression of intention—if such it is—be taken as decisive? We can help ourselves to answer this question by examining briefly what Joseph Kerman says of it at the beginning and the end of his careful analysis of the movement. Kerman says at the outset, "we scarcely need hints of representationalism to understand that he [Beethoven] felt he was trafficking with raw emotionality here." And, having completed a straightforward formal analysis of the movement, without introducing either expressive or representational terms at all, he reverts to the question of representation again, concluding:

> To sound the true note of tragedy which he seems clearly to have wanted here, Beethoven had to feel differently, not only to write differently. He stayed too close to a sentimental image of the star-crossed lovers of Verona, I have hazarded, but I am not suggesting that the image served him as anything more than a sort of externalization or excuse. The essential trouble had to do not with representation but with his own expressive resource. It was not external but internal, not literary or mythic but—need it be said?—musical.[3]

A number of dark sayings here I am not prepared to comment on, but one thing, I think, comes through with absolute clarity. Kerman rejects out of hand, without even the hint of an argument, a representational gloss of the movement, even though he is well aware of the evidence connecting it with *Romeo and Juliet*. It is as if he were saying, "This is just common sense, and good musical sense"; and with that I heartily agree.

Second, Kerman suggests that what the movement does contain, of the *Romeo and Juliet* theme, is not its program but its expressive qualities, at least as Beethoven understood them (which, Kerman more than hints, is a defective understanding). It is expressive of tragic and somewhat overwrought

3. Ibid., pp. 36, 41–42.

emotions. This, Kerman claims, we have no need of Beethoven's expressed intentions to reveal. We have no need of "hints of representationalism" to read in the music its "raw emotionality": the music tells all. And if Beethoven has failed, in the last analysis (as Kerman thinks, to a certain extent, he has), it is not a failure to deal adequately with a representational problem; rather, the problem was, "need it be said?—musical."

Now I am not, of course, suggesting that because one musical commentator ignores Beethoven's intention to represent, or perhaps discounts the evidence as evidence of such an intention (more of that in a moment), this must be how such things usually go. But I do suggest that there does not seem to be any pressing need to take such apparent expressions of intention as conclusive. A species of musical common sense tells us to ignore these obiter dicta, the common coin of program notes, when circumstances warrant our doing so.

What are the circumstances that warrant us to continue to read the second movement of Op. 18, No. 1, as pure music, Beethoven's apparent intention to the contrary notwithstanding? This movement occurs in what had, by Haydn's and Mozart's time, become the customary manner for pure instrumental music. It is a movement in a string quartet, one of the paradigms of pure music. It is a slow movement with no descriptive title, save for tempo and expression indications, occurring just where a slow movement can be expected, that is to say, the second movement. The quartet is one of the now customary collection of six, the collection being titled with nothing more than "Op. 18," the quartet with the equally laconic "No. 1." It is a movement, to be sure, redolent, almost extravagantly so, with expressive properties. But such properties alone can hardly warrant the conclusion that it is programmatic. Thus all of the "cues" we are given suggest pure music, music alone; and the movement fully sustains formal analysis, as well as "imageless" listening, without remainder or lack.

Here, of course, we face philosophical dangers similar to the ones we faced in ignoring Honegger's explicitly stated intention *not* to represent. If Beethoven tells us this movement is intended to be a representation of *Romeo and Juliet,* who are we to say nay? Who should know better than the Master?

I cited the case of Kerman, and I could have cited the case of Joseph de Marliave before him, who mentions the connection to *Romeo and Juliet* (in a footnote) only to ignore it in his analysis (except for a hint at the end),[4] merely to show that perfectly reputable and (in the case of Kerman) even distinguished practitioners of musical analysis and criticism will ignore such possible external evidence of composers' intentions if the music itself does not support it. And if one takes representation to be, as I think we must, in aesthetic contexts, a success concept, this attitude need cause us no feeling of paradox: an intention ignored in the face of recalcitrant music may be viewed as simply an intention that has failed.

One can, of course, claim here, as in the previous case, that we have something other than what appears to be the intention expressed. Kerman, I think, may be saying something like this, as there is the hint that what he takes the evidence to show is either Beethoven's intention merely as regards the expressive properties of the movement, which neither Kerman (apparently) nor I (definitely) take to be representational; or, rather, as no intention at all but a statement of Beethoven's inspiration, which need never, in the event, have become a part of the work.

In any case, it is not my wish, as I have said, to pursue the question of intention to the bitter end. What I have tried to do,

4. Joseph de Marliave, *Beethoven's Quartets,* trans. Hilda Andrews (New York, 1961), pp. 8–10. In a passage that could only, I think, have been written with prior knowledge of Beethoven's statement and jottings on the sketch, not surely by mere acquaintance with the music, Marliave concludes, "A light breath still flutters in the triplets of the first violin in the last four bars, and then the song dies into a sombre gloom where one feels the weight of an endless grief" (p. 9). But this remains, nevertheless, an expressive characterization, not a representational or programmatic one.

with these examples, is merely to suggest that music alone cannot be defined in terms of the intentions of composers alone, if only because, one way or the other, we do not seem willing to allow composers' intentions to override our strong musical impressions that a work is music alone or that it is not. And I will leave it at that.

Problems with the relevance of intentions, in our attempt to define music alone, are, of course, merely special cases of the general problem of intention in aesthetics. So these problems should be no surprise. To sum them up, they are: (1) We tend to argue from the music to the intention, inferring what the composer intended from what we find the music to be, rather than inferring what the music is, what we should take it to be, on the basis of what the composer intended; so that we cannot, in the end, be defining "music alone" as music intended by the composer to be music alone. (2) The well-documented intention of the composer to produce a piece that is not pure music will not, of itself, make us reject it as an example of pure music, which, of itself, defeats the notion that pure music is, by definition, music intended to be so. (3) Conversely, even the well-documented intention of the composer to write a piece of pure music will not, of itself, make it so, since we have such cases as *Pacific 231* in which representationality overcomes intention, again defeating the notion that music alone can be defined in terms of the composer's intentions. All in all, then, we seem to be finding that what determines our decisions is the music itself. What can sustain our interest as pure music, as music alone, is, ipso facto, music alone, the composer's intentions notwithstanding.

This opposite extreme will no doubt appeal to the inveterate seeker-after-definitions as a possible definition in its own right, avoiding the pitfalls of intentions while capturing some of our usage and intuitions. It will, for example, allow us to accommodate quite handily the "African mask problem," where a definition based on intentions will not. For on this definition it does not matter a whit that the person who made the African mask had no concept of a "work of art" and a fortiori, no intention to create one (understood under that description). The mask will sustain scrutiny and reward it handsomely when looked at as a piece of sculpture, and, on this definition, we need nothing more to constitute it "sculpture," where the maker's intention was "magic" or whatever. Likewise, no matter what the intentions of the Indian musicians who "compose" ragas, religious ecstasy, or whatever—for like the canzoni of Gabrieli, they were not meant for the recital hall or the recital hall mentality—the ragas can be attended to, with at least some aesthetic payoff, as one attends to such Western forms of music alone as, for example, the theme-and-variations. And, so the intentionless definition tells us, *if they can, they are.*

But the price one pays for this easy accommodation of non-Western musics and premodern instrumental pieces with the mainstream of Western instrumental music is a familiar and heavy one. The net it casts is all too wide; the definition is "oceanic." Not only will all music bear some interest as music alone, so will lots of (prima facie) nonmusic as well: bird "songs," natural sounds, mechanical noises, language, and so forth.

Now there is no harm in saying that we can, at times, hear the noises birds make *as* music—*as if* they were music. But if that is the case, we hear them *as if* they had certain syntactical properties: we hear them as "melodies," with implied "harmonic" structure; with "cadences" and "direction"; as "resolving [implicit] dissonances," and the like. And that is alright too, just as long as we remain squarely within the "as if" mode. For to say we hear bird songs *as if* they had syntactical properties is *not* to ascribe syntactical properties to them, any more than we are describing a monster when we say of someone that it is *as if* he had eyes in the back of his head. However, as soon as we take being able to hear bird noises *as* music to imply that therefore they *are* music, we are saying that they *literally* have syntactic properties; and *that* is a conceptual impossibility. A natural object *cannot,* as a matter of logic, have syntactic properties, whether it is a bird's "song" or anything else (unless you include human language and thought among the stock of "natural objects"). The winds and the tides may, by chance, produce on the beach an arrangement of pebbles that looks like letters spelling out a well-formed, grammatically correct English sentence. But it cannot be one: it cannot possess the syntactic and semantic properties that English sentences possess. Only language users can, under the proper circumstances, impart to "objects" real syntactic and semantic properties. However much bird "songs" may sound like music, they cannot *be* music—unless, of course, we ascribe to birds a mental life comparable to our own, which few of us will want to do. This may seem a philosopher's quibble. But as we will have later occasion to see, it is on the contrary, of the deepest significance for our understanding of music.

The fact that these rather tentative forays into the "definition" of music alone have all gone awry should in no way be taken as showing the futility or impossibility of the task. But I do want to make the point that it would be without purpose to pursue definition here. For the whole question of "defining" music alone, like that of compositional intent, is just a special case of a more general question in the philosophy of art, namely, the definition of "art" itself. This question has been canvassed very thoroughly in other places. One does not go to a book on the aesthetics of music to see rehashed again, in the form of a special case, a question one can find treated more thoroughly, and more appropriately, in a general work on the philosophy of art. So we can return now, somewhat more enlightened, I hope, and more ready to accept it, to the modest and perhaps lazy expedient of "defining" our subject matter by ostension.

We will have to take as a given that works such as Bach's *Well-Tempered Clavier,* Beethoven's C♯-Minor String Quartet, Brahms's Fourth Symphony, and Schoenberg's Woodwind Quintet are music alone, pure instrumental music. Anything else "enough" like them is pure music as well. We will have to be satisfied with a class that has very vague outlines indeed. I do not even know whether I can say that such "hard core" examples of the instrumental literature as Bach's "Brandenburg" Concertos (written for "social" musicmaking), Handel's *Music for the Royal Fireworks* (written as part of what we would now call a "mixed media" event), Mozart's serenades and divertimenti (dinner music), Beethoven's *Egmont* or *Coriolanus* overtures (incidental music for the theatre) really count as music alone, in the full-blown sense, or whether we simply treat them as—as if—music alone. Are we on a slippery slope that leads from Bach to bird songs? Perhaps, all things considered (or considered "too curiously"), there is *no* case of pure, unadulterated music alone. These vagaries we will have to put up with in the interest of a greater good. And it will of necessity be no concern to me whether the conclusions reached here are about what happens when we have appropriate encounters with music alone or about what happens when we have such encounters with what we can successfully treat *as* music alone. Short of a definition of "music alone" family resemblances are what we must settle for. And we are, here and now, short of a definition.

Given, then, that we will have to examine pure music without a definition, how can we characterize our enterprise? The subtitle of this book, *Philosophical Reflections on the Purely Musical Experience,* is intended to help us in that direction. For we do have central cases, whether we have a definition or not, and it is the *experience* of those central cases I propose to examine.

Let us suppose we can agree, as I think we can, that a fairly large number of instrumental works of the last three hundred fifty years are pure instrumental music, what I have been calling music alone, regardless of the fact that some of them were not intended only or entirely in that way. By examining how we appreciate, understand, and enjoy such works, and what we appreciate, understand, and enjoy in them, we will be limning an outline of what I call the purely musical experience.

Now, of course, other works besides what we agree are core instances of music alone can sustain, to varying degrees, the kind of attention that characterizes the purely musical experience. So the purely musical experience—appreciation, understanding, enjoyment—can be got from works other than works of pure music. I can have the purely musical experience from a Schubert song, a Mozart aria, or the *Symphonie fantastique,* without its implying that any of those is music alone—which, manifestly, none of them is. Now, of course, I am not saying that is the best way to appreciate such works, any more than the best way to appreciate an African mask is to contemplate it, hanging on a wall, in the same spirit as one might appreciate an antique bust or Michelangelo's *David.* Indeed, as it might be construed a misunderstanding of the African mask to view it solely as sculpture, in the manner of Phidias or Michelangelo, so it would certainly be a misunderstanding to know the *Marriage of Figaro* only in a wind band arrangement or the *Symphonie fantastique* without any acquaintance with its program or movement titles. All I am saying is that the mask can afford the kind of appreciation and enjoyment afforded by Phidias and Michelangelo; and songs without words or symphonies without their programs can afford the kind of appreciation and enjoyment that music alone affords. (To what degree is another matter.)

Failure to take on the formidable task of defining "music alone" lays me open, the wary reader will no doubt observe, to the obvious danger of begging that very important question or arguing in a circle. For if I choose paradigms of music alone without defining the genre and then, having analyzed what I call the "purely musical experience" as the experience afforded by those works, define music alone as the music which affords that experience, it may well be suspected that I chose my examples to fit a preconceived notion of what the purely musical experience is, thus getting the inevitable but question-begging result of a perfect fit between what *I* call the purely musical experience and what *I* call examples of music alone.

There is, no doubt, some bootstrapping going on here. One cannot begin with a *tabula rasa;* and, of course, I had, before I started this investigation, some notion of what the purely musical experience would turn out to be. (I have, after all, some direct acquaintance with it.) But if this is bootstrapping, it is a benign form of the thing. One cannot ask a sensible question, in a philosophical inquiry or anywhere else, without having some idea of the answer. Be that as it may, it can hardly be said that the examples of music alone I have selected as paradigms—such works as Beethoven's Op. 131 or *The Well-Tempered Clavier*—are quirky, or personal, or suggest some bizarre and theoretically motivated method of choice. Were I to have selected as paradigms such things as titled harpsichord pieces, with no *obvious* representational qualities, by eighteenth-century French composers, some would say that the titles are irrelevant and the works pure instrumental music, others that the titles *must* be relevant, the apparent absence of representational qualities notwithstanding, and the works, therefore, not music alone. Were I to have chosen examples from the various genres of instrumental music meant to serve extramusical functions—music for dancing, or for ceremonial occasions, or for worship—it might be charged that the parameters of appreciation of such works, their standards of success, go beyond the purely musical, even though the works possess no other but purely musical parameters. I have, on the contrary, been extremely careful in my choice of paradigms, and those I have chosen seem to me beyond controversy. I certainly may be mistaken about how I analyze our experience of these works; but that I am mistaken, or overly influenced by theory, in calling them examples of pure music would suggest the same degree of unintelligibility or conceptual impossibility attaching to the denial that the plays of Shakespeare or the paintings of Rembrandt are works of art.

Here, then, is the general outline of my procedure. I wish to analyze what I call the purely musical experience. This experience I characterize in terms of how we enjoy, appreciate, and understand certain musical works of the past (almost) four hundred years. I cannot state, in terms of necessary and sufficient conditions, or anything like that, what qualifies as a work of pure music or what I call music alone. But I can identify such works, on grounds independent of what will emerge as the purely musical experience, by appealing to the core of the instrumental repertoire, agreed upon by the musical community at large to be the paradigms of contentless instrumental music, at least as that characterization is generally understood *before* one might on theoretical grounds claim that "pure" music *also* has content (in some theoretical sense of that word).

The procedure is neither circular nor question-begging. Nor is it logically hard-edged or rigorous. To those who are looking for such qualities, I would certainly suggest a different book—and, indeed, a different subject as well.

CHAPTER 3

The Stimulation Model

worst model

If we date the beginnings of the modern instrumental music tradition from the end of the sixteenth century, it should come as no surprise to us that the beginnings of a philosophical account of music alone are found in the seventeenth. And because, until the time of Haydn and Mozart, pure instrumental music, with a few notable exceptions, was never the primary business of a composer but—composing *being* a *business*—always something of a sideline, philosophical theories of pure music were themselves fragmentary and underdeveloped, the far more pressing and important issues revolving around music with text, be it operatic or religious. Composers were employed to write for the church, or for the stage, or for the private worship of kings and princes. Instrumental music was the *pièce d'occasion,* the not too frequent commission, the teaching material. And so, when pure music is discussed by philosophers and the "philosophically inclined," in the seventeenth and early eighteenth centuries, it is an afterthought or an appendage to a more thoroughgoing discussion of what really matters in music: the musical setting of texts and instrumental music as part of a dramatic representation.

The most clearly discernible account in early modern philosophy of the pure musical experience, our appreciation of and pleasure in the pure musical parameters, is what I call the "stimulation model." Baldly, it takes pure music to be a physical stimulus that, by interacting with our sense organs and, through them, the rest of our auditory apparatus, puts us in a pleasurable state. It is directly analogous to the way wine intoxicates us and sugar pleases the taste but wormwood doesn't. It is an utterly hopeless view, but more than merely antiquarian interest impels me to take it up. For it is my experience that a surprising number of well-educated and musically sophisticated people still hold such a view, believing, somehow, that when it is stated, not of course in seventeenth-century terms but in those of modern neurophysiology, it is the "scientifically correct" account of the matter.

Now, of course, if one chooses the stimulation of alcohol, a narcotic drug, or anything else of the kind as the reigning metaphor for the stimulation model of the pure musical experience, various possibilities will immediately come to the reader's mind. A drug may, in one sense of "stimulate," cause changes in the body of which the partaker is not aware; that clearly is the means to the desired end, whatever the drug. Or it may stimulate, which is to say arouse, conscious intentional states such as the "pipe dream" of the opium addict. But where the stimulus model begins to flirt with such experiences, it is becoming quite another kind of account, imparting content of a nonmusical kind to the musical experience; and that is the subject for another chapter. Various other possibilities exist, and it is not clear how precise any of the early stimulus models were about what they were claiming for the purely musical experience. What does seem dominant, however, is the idea that the experience of music consists in the stimulation of a pleasurable state, perhaps something between the general state of well-being sometimes described by addicts and alcoholics and locatable physical pleasure. I say "something between" these two since the pleasure seems in a way physical, located, as it is, in the sense of hearing but yet not locatable in the way in which pure sexual pleasure (say) may be located in a particular organ or place on the body.

One very distinguished proponent, in the seventeenth century, of what I call the stimulation model of the pure musical experience was René Descartes. Not only did he present the view explicitly in his early *Compendium of Music* (1618, first published posthumously in 1650), but he provided, in his *Passions of the Soul* (1649), the foundations, in psychological theory, for later versions. It seems inevitable, therefore, that we begin with Descartes. And what he says, in the beginning of his *Compendium of Music,* is this: "The basis of music is sound; its aim is to please and to arouse various emotions in us."[1]

What should be noted straightaway is that in Descartes, as in all of the early accounts of pure music, the notion that music stimulates us pleasurably is never very far from the equally ubiquitous notion that music arouses emotions in us: puts us in emotional states. The two notions are really parts of the same theory: the theory that our experience of pure music is simply the process of being stimulated pleasurably by musical sound. For the arousing of emotions is merely *another* way, and perhaps the most important way, on these early views, that music has of stimulating us pleasurably. This is why Descartes immediately adds, in the sentence following the one we have just quoted: "Melodies can be at the same time sad and enjoyable; nor is this so unique, for in the same way writers of elegies and tragedies please us most the more sorrow they awaken in us."

Now the theory that music can arouse emotions in listeners has, of course, a busy life of its own, one quite independent of its life as part of the stimulation theory of music alone, and there are serious as well as well-known difficulties with it. These difficulties, along with the whole topic of "music and emotion" as it relates to the pure musical experience, will be

---

1. René Descartes, *Compendium of Music,* trans. Walter Robert, ed. Charles Kent (American Institute of Musicology, 1961), p. 11.

taken up later on. Our immediate object here is merely to get some idea how, on Descartes' view, music is supposed to arouse the emotions. For it is only in understanding this that we will be able to understand the logical form of the stimulation model and its failure.

Were the *Compendium of Music* the only work of Descartes' we possessed, we would be in a poor if not hopeless position to ascertain how he thought music stimulated either pleasure in general or emotional pleasure in particular. But with hindsight provided by the *Passions of the Soul,* and assuming that the theory of human emotions contained therein was already in place, at least in rough outline, in the early *Compendium of Music,* we can get a fair idea of Descartes' mechanism for musical stimulation; and "mechanism" certainly is the appropriate as well as significant word.

The crucial passage in the *Compendium,* for our understanding of how the mechanism of musical stimulation and arousal operates, is not concerned directly with these things; rather, it has to do with the effect of music on human *movement:* time-beating and dancing. But as we shall see in a moment, an application to it of the general principle of emotive arousal enunciated in the *Passions of the Soul* will yield directly the desired conclusion. The passage in question is this:

> [A]t the beginning of each measure the sound is produced more distinctly; singers and instrumentalists observe this instinctively, especially in connection with tunes to which we are accustomed to dance and sway. Here we accompany each beat of the music by a corresponding motion of our body; we are quite naturally impelled to do this by the music. For it is undoubtedly true that sound strikes all bodies on all sides. . . . Since this is so, and since, as we have said, the sound is emitted more strongly and clearly at the beginning of each measure, we must conclude that it has greater impact on our spirits, and that we are thus roused to motion.[2]

2. Ibid., pp. 14–15.

trying to Explain Descartes

The best way to understand this passage is to work backward. Descartes says that sounds have an impact on our "spirits": the louder the sound, the greater the impact. What are these "spirits"? Clearly they are the "animal spirits" of the *Passions of the Soul*—"esprits animaux" in the French version—that, on Descartes's view, are the direct physical causes of human emotions. The nerves, Descartes says, "are like little tubes which all come from the brain, and [which] like it, contain a certain very subtle air or wind which is called animal spirits." This "very subtle air or wind" moves in quite discrete and (so Descartes thought) clearly identifiable ways, causing the "passions of the soul" in all of their familiar particularity. He concludes, on this regard: "Having considered how the passions of the soul differ from all its other thoughts, it seems to me that we may generally define them as those perceptions, sensations or emotions of the soul which we refer specifically to it, and which are caused, maintained and fortified by some movement of the animal spirits."[3]

On Descartes' view, then, here is the way an emotion would standardly be aroused and what would transpire in its wake. Take, for instance, fear brought about by my perception of a charging rhino. I see the beast, put two and two together (very quickly, one hopes), and the animal spirits in my brain are thrown into that particular violent agitation which (in accordance, presumably, with a psychophysical law) produces the subjective feeling of fear in me. In the same process, the animal spirits in my nerve-tubes, connecting my brain to my legs, are set in an identical kind of violent motion that, we must supposed, is peculiarly suited to making my legs move in such a way as to produce running. And off I go.

Let me add one more passage from the *Compendium,* and we will be in a position to grasp what Descartes is up to there. He says, right after the passage on how music rouses us to phys-

3. René Descartes, *The Passions of the Soul,* in *Essential Works of Descartes,* trans. Lowell Bair (New York, 1966), p. 111 (Part I, Article 7), pp. 121–122 (Part I, Article 27). The translation is of the French version.

ical motion, but without explicitly suggesting any connection, "As regards the various emotions which music can arouse by employing various meters, I will say that in general a slower pace arouses in us quieter feelings such as languor, sadness, fear, pride, etc. A faster pace arouses faster emotions, such as joy, etc."[4]

Let us ask, now, in light of what we know about Descartes' theory of emotion and the relation of emotion to behavior, how music causes us to move. Then we will be able to go on to an explanation of how it *moves* us emotionally.

Descartes says that music causes me to move my foot—that is, beat time—at the beginning of the measure because the music is played louder at that point, having an effect on my animal spirits. Now the *ordinary* way my animal spirits make me move—remember the charging rhino—is through perceiving that something threatening, or beneficial, or whatever, is happening; having my animal spirits set in motion in some distinctive way, thus arousing the appropriate emotion; and that, in turn, again through the distinctive motion of the animal spirits, causing me to flee, or approach, or whatever else might be the sensible thing in the circumstances. So what Descartes seems to be saying is that music can intervene in this process and make the animal spirits do their act *without* my perceiving charging rhinos or good things happening but in some different way, as a neurologist (on a more up-to-date model) might tickle the part of my brain responsible for vision, causing me to "see" a red flash without the aid of my eyes at all. (It is the same explanation Descartes himself used in the *Meditations* to account for the pain the amputee feels "in" his missing foot: the so-called "phantom limb" phenomenon.)

But now we can see directly that the very same process by which the music makes me move my foot must, of necessity, arouse emotion in me as well. For the nerve is a conduit that goes in two directions, to my foot and to my brain, and it is

4. Descartes, *Compendium of Music*, p. 15.

full of a fluid or pneumatic medium that, when set in motion, causes me to have emotions. So if the music sets the medium in motion *anywhere* in the conduit, then to the extent it will cause my foot to move at one end, that same motion will also propagate as a matter of course to the other end—the brain end, that is to say—and the emotion appropriate to the particular motion of the animal spirits in question will perforce be aroused. This being the case, it is perfectly clear why Descartes says, in the passage just quoted, that a slower musical pace will arouse quieter feelings, a faster pace more violent ones. For he must be thinking it understood that music arouses the emotions by setting the animal spirits in motion. Presumably, the gentler emotions are caused by gentler movements of the spirits, gentler movements of the spirits by gentler music; the converse, of course, is also true, so that violent music will cause violent motions of the *esprits animaux,* which in their turn will cause violent emotions. That, in essence, is Descartes' view, given the assumption, which seems altogether plausible, that the general outlines of his psychological theory were already understood implicitly in the *Compendium of Music.*

We must be reminded at this point that the arousal of emotions was not, on Descartes' view, an end in itself but a means to the general end of musical pleasure. How does the arousing of emotions by music please us (a question all the more necessary to ask when we observe, as Descartes did not fail to do, that some emotions, under some conditions, are distinctly unpleasant)? Descartes, as far as I know, never gave an answer to this question. But an answer generally accepted by eighteenth-century writers on the subject was already being adumbrated in the late seventeenth century, receiving, I think, its best-known formulation in the Abbé Du Bos's popular and influential book *Réflexions critiques sur la poësie et sur la peinture* (1719). It is an answer, I suggest, not inconsistent with Descartes' views and would have been perhaps, congenial to him. So I round out the Cartesian account of music as pleasurable stimulation by appending to it Du Bos's explanation for how the arousing of emotions, particularly the unpleasant ones, pleases us.

The answer is simply that emotive arousal by artistic means provides the mind with pleasurable activity. "The soul," says Du Bos, "hath its wants no less than the body; and one of the greatest wants of man is to have his mind incessantly occupied. The heaviness which quickly attends the inactivity of the mind, is a situation so very disagreeable to a man, that he frequently chuses to expose himself to the most painful exercises, rather than be troubled with it."[5] One of these painful exercises, on Du Bos's view, is the exercise provided the mind by the arousal of painful emotions. Therein lies our propensity for enjoying even the most hair-raising dramatic spectacles, with all of the attendant terrors we may experience in observing them; therein, too, lies our propensity for enjoying the emotion-charged art of music, even when the emotions experienced are the ones we think likely, under many circumstances, to be unpleasant and (therefore) to be avoided.

Here, then, is Descartes' account of pure musical pleasure stated in general outline. Music is a stimulus directly to the animal spirits. By stimulating them to motion, it pleases us (apparently) in two ways. First, merely in the process, I presume, of setting the spirits in motion (for, as you will remember, Descartes distinguished between the power of music to please *sans phrase* and its power to please through emotive arousal); but second, and more significantly, in the process of arousing emotions, *by* setting the spirits in motion. The pleasure of emotive arousal is the pleasure of mental "exercise," perhaps, as later writers took it to be; and just to make things neat and tidy, let's say (on absolutely no textual evidence at all) that *both* musical stimulation *sans phrase and* musical stimulation through emotive arousal are, at their root, pleasures of

5. [Jean-Baptiste] Abbé Du Bos, *Critical Reflections on Poetry, Painting, and Music,* trans. Thomas Nugent (London, 1748), 1:5.

mental exercise: for our purposes, the point need not be pursued further.

Now it makes absolutely no difference to us that Descartes' model of musical stimulation is based on an absolutely false theory of human physiology, on an absolutely false theory of emotions, and on the absolutely false assumption (as I shall argue in due course) that music is able, in its normal aesthetic functioning, to arouse such emotions as love, hate, hope, anger, and fear. What does matter is that Descartes thought of pure music, music alone, as a stimulus to pleasure much in the way that wine is a stimulus to intoxication: that is to say, through the operation of various causal mechanisms and laws, the one results from the other. And no matter what streamlined mechanisms and laws one might suggest to replace Descartes' horse-and-buggy "neurology," the stimulus model remains hopeless. To see just why, it is instructive to listen to what Descartes' great near-contemporary, Leibniz, had to say; for the view was already beginning to show signs of breaking down even in Leibniz's ingenious effort to bolster it up. The way he expressed himself in his most familiar and intriguing characterization of music alone strongly suggests that Leibniz had doubts of which, perhaps, he was only dimly aware—but doubts that were right on target.

In the famous passage from the "Principles of Nature and Grace," Leibniz writes that "even the pleasures of sense are reducible to intellectual pleasures, known confusedly. Music charms us, although its beauty consists only in the agreement of numbers and in the counting, which we do not perceive but which the soul nevertheless continues to carry out, of the beats or vibrations of sounding bodies which coincides at certain intervals."[6] Now without delving into the significance of this passage for the Leibnizian philosophy of art, as developed by Leibniz himself in various places and later by Alexander

6. Gottfried Wilhelm Leibniz, "Principles of Nature and Grace," in *Philosophical Papers and Letters,* trans. and ed. Leroy E. Loemker (Chicago, 1956), 2:1042.

Baumgarten systematically, and ignoring, too, the reverberations of Pythagorean music theory and "number mysticism,"
neither being relevant to our present concerns, we can see
directly, I think, that Leibniz's intriguing observation here is,
in a significant sense, divided against itself. On the one hand,
Leibniz, like Descartes, seems to be saying that pure music,
music alone, is a simple pleasure of sense: a titillation of the
sense organ as "mindless" as the taste of honey or the pleasing
warmth of a fire after a walk in the snow. But why, then, the
perennially fascinating image of the soul, unperceived by us,
"counting" the musical "numbers"? Because, I would urge,
Leibniz believes pure music to possess an aesthetically significant property that cannot be dealt with on the stimulation
model: a property that must be cognized to be enjoyed. It was
natural, I suppose, that the philosopher–mathematician should
have bought into the ancient and medieval doctrine of music as
the mathematical art; and once he had done so, the move
seems inevitable toward a cognitive account of musical appreciation. For how else can we suppose the mathematical "properties" to function, in any interesting way, except by being
grasped by a mind? The senses cannot "count"; counting is an
intellectual occupation. Hence Leibniz was forced to imagine
some kind of calculating "homunculus" within the human
mind, tolling the musical numbers. Mathematics requires a
mind.

But Leibniz was fallen between two stools, because he also
brought into the stimulus model of musical enjoyment. For
pure music, music alone, being a "contentless," nonrepresentational art form, hardly seemed other than a pure stimulus to
the senses. (What was there to think about, to be conscious
of?) Thus the musical "counting" of the soul must remain an
unconscious process that somehow accounted for the pleasure
of the musical stimulus, through the presence of the mathematical properties, without compromising the basically
"mindless" character of the stimulation model. Whatever
thinking was going on must be unconscious thinking, because

from the auditor's point of view all that was happening—all that he or she was aware of—was being stimulated to pleasure by a physical medium possessing neither semantic nor representational content.

Forget that Leibniz's "unconscious counting" is a fantasy. Forget that he had not entirely given up the stimulation model but had plumped for a very implausible compromise. Forget that the cognitive property of music he picked, the "agreement of numbers," was an age-old trap that people are still falling into.[7] But *don't* forget that Leibniz must have at least had a glimmering of the truth. And the truth is: music is not a stimulus object but a cognitive one. - *ala Langer*

One thing should be clear straightaway. If music merely stimulated pleasure the way drugs stimulate euphoria, it would be impossible to make any sense at all out of what Tibby is doing, "who is profoundly versed in counterpoint, and holds the full score open on his knee." What would being profoundly versed in *anything* have to do with musical enjoyment if music were a sonic drug? The pharmacologist who is profoundly versed in the ways in which heroin affects the brain does not get a different or more enjoyable "high" from it than the neighborhood addict who knows nothing at all about how the substance works. But Tibby, we must suppose, is not profoundly versed in the way music gives us a "high," as the pharmacologist is profoundly versed in the way heroin does. His knowledge of counterpoint and ability to read the score are enabling him to perceive *that* certain things are going on in the music, and his enjoyment of the music is the enjoyment *of* perceiving just those things under those descriptions. The

7. The times I have been told by scientists that music is "mathematical," or that they like Bach because he is "so mathematical," are uncountable. Perhaps this misunderstanding is responsible for the phenomenon that C. P. Snow observed in the famous "Two Cultures" lecture where, after noting the paucity of art in the scientists' world, he added: "with the exception, an important exception, of music." *The Two Cultures; and A Second Look* (Cambridge, 1983), p. 13.

counterpoint doesn't cause Tibby to have pleasure the way chemical *xyz* causes the addict to have a "high." It causes pleasure *in* the perceiving and the being aware. The music is not a stimulus for him: it is an object of perception and cognition, which understanding opens up for his appreciation.

All very well for Tibby, you may reply; Tibby is just that kind of person who enjoys music cerebrally. But we should not generalize from one type of listener to all. What about Margaret? She has no knowledge of counterpoint, nor can she follow the score of Beethoven's Fifth Symphony. "Margaret, who can only see music . . . ," is also a listener, and much more like the rest of us than the learned Tibby. There seems no compelling reason to believe that she understands music as an object of cognition. What does she understand, after all? She has no knowledge of music. Perhaps, then, the stimulation model may not be for Tibby. Why could it not be for Margaret?

It would be getting ahead of myself to try to answer this question here and now. But I will, indeed, be claiming, as the argument progresses, that music is an object of cognition not only for Tibby but for Margaret, too, and even for Mrs. Munt all the while she is "mindlessly" tapping her foot when the tunes come. Where "music" is pure pleasurable stimulation, as perhaps it is in the case of a three-day-old infant, "instinctively" moving to its rhythm as one of my nieces used to do (who now shows no particular talent for music), it is simply not "music." This is not a limiting case of the musical experience; it is not a case at all. And if it is where the musical experience "originates," which I don't necessarily deny, it would be no more than an obvious instance of the genetic fallacy to insist that *therefore* it *must* be music.

No: the stimulation model of pure musical enjoyment is a nonstarter. It has *almost* everything wrong. But it does have *one thing* right, as we will see in the next chapter.

CHAPTER 4

Helen's Way

What the stimulation theory of music alone gets total-ly wrong is the kind of perceptual object music must be. For, as I shall argue, music is an object of perceptual consciousness. Even at the most unsophisticated, "mindless" level of musical appreciation, music is not physical stimulus to pleasure but perceived and cognized object for the ear, always understood under some description or other, no matter how vague and how vaguely present to awareness. Musical pleasure is pleasure *in* something heard and conceived. It is, to use the language of contemporary analytic philosophy of mind, an "intentional" object of consciousness; and, as Roger Scruton writes, "Understanding music is a special case of intentional understanding."[1]

The most obvious way of construing music intentionally is to construe it as representational. In the eighteenth century, when music was first beginning to be thought of as one of the fine arts, this had the added advantage of providing a single principle—namely, *mimesis*—which could be seen to bind all of the arts together into one enterprise: holding up the mirror

---

1. Roger Scruton, "Understanding Music," in *The Aesthetic Understanding* (London, 1983), p. 78.

to nature. Indeed, it seems probable that the latter motive rather than the former was the operative one. But it is the former that concerns us here.

Clearly, there is no way of construing a representational object, *qua* representational, as anything but an object of cognition; so in construing music as a representational art, one ipso facto takes the musical object beyond the mere stimulus to pleasure of the stimulation model and places it squarely in the realm of intentionality. In that, if in nothing else, the representational model of music alone is a distinct improvement. But, it hardly need be said, it has problems of its own; indeed, on first blush the theory seems not merely false but absurd. For how can an explanation of music alone possibly be framed in terms of musical representation? Music alone is pure, contentless music; representation, by its very nature, is content-laden. Representation must be *of something*. So it seems a flat-out contradiction in terms to say that music alone can be explained in terms of its representational properties. By hypothesis, it has none.

The first obstacle to overcome in any representational analysis of pure instrumental music, then, is the initial charge of prima facie absurdity. That charge had already been at least tacitly recognized and answered in the eighteenth century.

At one level of analysis, of course, one wants to make a straightforward distinction between instrumental music that is representational and instrumental music that is pure, contentless abstraction, between, for example, the concerti of Vivaldi's that represent the seasons and Bach's "Brandenburg" Concertos that represent nothing at all and are paradigms of music alone.

But now, how is it that those very "Brandenburg" Concertos whose pure, contentless character is being contrasted with the obviously representational character of Vivaldi's *Seasons* are also to be construed as deriving their effect, *qua* pure instrumental music, from representational features of their own? The answer must be that there is some deeper representational layer, beneath the superficial surface of apparent nonrepresentationality, accounting for the pleasure we take in what we hear as pure musical parameters. And indeed, since all music, even the most frankly representational, has pure musical parameters as well—harmonic, rhythmic, contrapuntal, melodic—it follows that all music, of the kind we are talking about, has a deep layer of representationality, whether there is surface representationality as in the case of Vivaldi's *Seasons* or not, as in the case of the "Brandenburgs." This is a familiar philosophical strategy. One cannot help being reminded, for example, of the psychological egoist, who wants, like the rest of us, to distinguish between selfish and unselfish acts and yet wants also to maintain that this distinction to the contrary notwithstanding, all acts are at some deeper level motivated by self-interest.

In the eighteenth century, at the point where pure instrumental music was beginning to be a center of attraction and not merely a sideshow, the most frequently cited object of representation at the deep layer was the human voice. But the end was not representation *simpliciter;* rather, representation of the human voice was to be representation of passionate human utterance, and this in turn was meant, by a kind of sympathetic reverberation, to arouse in the listener whatever passion the represented voice was represented as expressing. The arousing of the passion itself was either left as a self-evidently pleasurable result or, as in the case of Du Bos and others, explained in terms of the pleasure of mental "exercise" (or some other such psychological principle). This means of producing "pure" musical pleasure was, by the way, seldom if ever appealed to in isolation but usually in tandem with some kind of stimulation model. Francis Hutcheson is a case in point. Having in one place provided an explanation of musical pleasure in "harmony" in pure stimulus terms, he reverts, in another, to a representation model of the kind just outlined above for melody, stating:

There is also another charm in music to various persons, which is distinct from harmony and is occasioned by its raising agreeable passions. The human voice is obviously varied by all the stronger passions: now when our ear discerns any resemblance between the air of a tune, whether sung or played upon an instrument, either in its time, or modulation, or any other circumstances, to the sound of the human voice in any passion, we shall be touched by it in a very sensible manner, and have melancholy, joy, gravity, thoughtfulness excited in us by a sort of *sympathy* or *contagion*.[2]

Hutcheson was writing in the first quarter of the century. In the last quarter, Thomas Reid was still mining the same vein, albeit somewhat more ambitiously and with considerably greater sophistication. Hutcheson presents a two-pronged theory in which only one of the pure musical parameters, that of melody, is given a representational accounting. The reason for his doing so is not far to seek. The obvious analogue in music of vocal utterance, is the melodic line, which, in solo song and aria would, of course, be another vocal utterance: that is to say, singing. The notion that the melodic line of an instrumental work is a representation of passionate vocal utterance appears to be a vestige of a theory that flowered in the seventeenth century to the effect that the vocal lines of *stile rappresentativo,* recitative, and aria are representational in that way. The theory is, needless to say, far more plausible when applied to vocal music than to instrumental, and it appeared far more adequate in an age in which vocal music was at center stage, instrumental music a minor art. But Hutcheson must surely have felt, even if he did not express, the monstrous implausibility of applying such a representational theory to anything but the melodic line of an instrumental composition (or a vocal one, for that matter); and so must have felt obliged to

2. Francis Hutcheson, *Inquiry Concerning Beauty, Order, Harmony, Design,* ed. Peter Kivy (The Hague, 1973), pp. 46–47, 81.

provide another explanation, the stimulus model, to explain the effect of the other, nonmelodic musical parameters, which he placed under the rather uninformative rubric "harmony."

Reid, however, was of sterner philosophical stuff, and he made an attempt (at least as I read him) to interpret even the nonmelodic parameters representationally. Of melody, he has much the same thing to say as Hutcheson: "To me it seems, that every strain in melody that is agreeable, is an imitation of the tones of the human voice in the expression of some sentiment or passion, or an imitation of some other object in nature; and that music, as well as poetry, is an imitative art."[3] But as to what he, like Hutcheson, calls "harmony," and what we should take, I think, to cover both harmonic and contrapuntal polyphony, Reid does not take the easy and well-trodden path of the stimulation model. Rather, he tries to gather "harmony" too into a representational account, although the tentative character of the explanation is underscored by Reid's obvious reluctance to use the word "imitation" here as he does with regard to melody.

Reid begins his account of "harmony" by suggesting that musical terminology in this regard is parasitic on nonmusical discourse. "In harmony, the very names of concord and discord are metaphorical, and suppose some analogy between the relations of sound, to which they are figuratively applied, and the relations of minds and affections, which they originally and properly signify." It is, I suggest, not a very great step, indeed no step at all, in Reid's text from saying that relations of sound bear some "analogy" to minds and affections to saying that they represent them. This becomes even more apparent as Reid fleshes out the details of his scheme. It is conversation that, he thinks, music reflects; and conversation, like pure musical structure, displays, on Reid's view, concord,

3. Thomas Reid, *Essays on the Intellectual Powers in Man,* in *The Philosophical Works of Thomas Reid,* ed. Sir William Hamilton, 8th ed. (Edinburgh, 1895), 1:504.

discord, and resolution. In conversation, "when two or more persons, of a good voice and ear, converse together in amity and friendship, the tones of their different voices are concordant, but become discordant when they give vent to angry passions." And in conversation, as in music, the resolution of discord, the return to agreement, makes a welcome cadence. "When discord arises occasionally in conversation, but soon terminates in perfect amity, we receive more pleasure than from perfect unanimity. In like manner, in the harmony of music, discordant sounds are occasionally introduced, but it is always in order to give relish to the most perfect concord that follows." Reid concludes, on a somewhat tentative but nonetheless positive note, that *if* "these analogies between the harmony of a piece of music, and harmony in the intercourse of minds . . . have any just foundation, as they seem to me to have, they serve to account for the metaphorical application of the names of concord and discord to the relations of sounds; to account for the pleasure we have from harmony in music; and to shew, that the beauty of harmony is derived from the relation it has to agreeable affections of mind."[4]

The philosophical attempt to see the representational depth beneath the nonrepresentational surface of pure instrumental music was, then, already a going concern in the eighteenth century. But most of us know it, if we know it at all, through Schopenhauer, where the theory takes a distinctly metaphysical turn that makes its implausibility all the more apparent, although, at the same time, it reveals its raison d'être more fully. Schopenhauer, as is well-known, thought of the world as what he called an "objectification" of the "will": the will being not the human will, or the will of any nonhuman being, but a metaphysical "thing-in-itself," an ultimate reality lying beneath the "phenomena" of the world as we perceive and know them. Music, he thought, was somehow an icon of that

4. Ibid.

metaphysical will: a "copy" of the will itself, as he called it (in the translations both of Payne and of Haldane and Kamp).[5]

Schopenhauer went further, identifying various aspects of the harmonic music of his time with various aspects of the world. Thus: "I recognize in the deepest tones of harmony, in the ground-bass, the lowest grades of the will's objectification, inorganic nature, the mass of the planet." In the inner voices,

[handwritten margin note: look deep enough you'll find it]

> between the bass and the leading voice singing the melody, I recognize the whole gradation of Ideas in which the will objectifies itself. Those nearer to the bass are the lower of those grades, namely, the still inorganic bodies manifesting themselves, however, in many ways. Those that are higher represent to me the plant and animal worlds. The definite intervals of the scale are parallel to the definite grades of the will's objectification, the definite species in nature.

The diapason closes full in Man: "Finally, in the *melody,* in the high, singing, principal voice, leading the whole and progressing with unrestrained freedom, in the uninterrupted significant connexion of *one* thought from beginning to end, and expressing a whole, I recognize the highest grade of the will's objectification, the intellectual life and endeavour of man."[6]

Whatever we might think of Schopenhauer's metaphysical effusions, they are motivated by a far clearer perception than we get in Hutcheson or even in Reid of what problems call the representation theory of music alone into being. There is no doubt, to begin with, that Schopenhauer is well aware of the distinction I have been drawing in this chapter between surface and depth representation; for, without using those words or any like them, he draws the distinction nevertheless, and with concrete examples to back it up. The "analogy discovered by

5. Arthur Schopenhauer, *The World as Will and Representation,* trans. E. F. J. Payne (Indian Hills, Colo., 1958), 1:257, and *The World as Will and Idea,* trans. R. B. Haldane and J. Kemp, 4th ed. (London, 1896), 1:333.
6. *The World as Will and Representation,* 1:258, 259.

the composer," between music, the will, and its various objectifications, Schopenhauer writes,

> must come from the immediate knowledge of the inner nature of the world unknown to his faculty of reason; it cannot be an imitation brought about with conscious intention by means of concepts, otherwise the music does not express the inner nature of the will itself, but merely imitates its phenomenon inadequately. All really imitative music does this: for example, *The Seasons* by Haydn, also many passages of his *Creation,* where phenomena of the world of perception are directly imitated; also in all battle pieces.[7]

I pass over in silence the problematic of representing without "conscious intention," but I do want to pursue further the significance of the surface-depth distinction for Schopenhauer. As he is perfectly clear about the distinction, he is clear, too, about the necessity for making it. One very important thing about pure instrumental music impresses Schopenhauer and cries out for explanation. Without any apparent representational qualities, pure music profoundly moves us, much in the way, it would seem, as the other fine arts, the obviously representational ones, but, on Schopenhauer's view, even more deeply. This profundity, this intensity and depth of musical enjoyment, cannot, he thinks, be accounted for by anything like what I have been calling the stimulation model. His exemplar here is Leibniz's subliminal counting of the musical numbers; if, he argues, musical satisfaction were merely the result of enumeration, "it would inevitably be similar to that which we feel when a sum in arithmetic comes out right, and could not be that profound [musical] pleasure with which we see the deepest recesses of our nature find expression." But if, as Schopenhauer seems to think, the quality of musical pleasure is akin to that of the other fine arts only more intense; further, if the other fine arts produce pleasure through representation;

7. Ibid., 1:263–264.

and finally, since pure instrumental music displays no surface representation; there must, Schopenhauer insists, be some deeper level at which music is representational, although we do not realize it—some deeper metaphysical reality that it reveals. And so, Schopenhauer argues,

> That in some sense music must be related to the world as the depiction to the thing depicted, as the copy to the original, we can infer from the analogy with the remaining arts, to all of which this character is peculiar; from their effect on us, it can be inferred that that of music is of the same nature, only stronger, more rapid, more necessary and infallible. Further, its imitative reference to the world must be very profound, infinitely true, and really striking, since it is instantly understood by everyone, and presents a certain infallibility by the fact that its form can be reduced to quite definite rules expressible in numbers, from which it cannot possibly depart without entirely ceasing to be music. Yet the point of comparison between music and the world, the regard in which it stands to the world in the relation of a copy, or a repetition, is very obscure. Men have practised music at all times without being able to give an account of this; content to understand it immediately, they renounce any abstract conception of this direct understanding itself.[8]

I have not trotted out Hutcheson, Reid, and Schopenhauer on musical representation merely as philosophical museum pieces. Rather, I have been attempting to establish that there is a philosophical tradition of such musical understanding pretty much throughout the modern history of music alone, which is to say, from the emancipation of pure music as an art form in the eighteenth century. And before I come to examine these views more fully, I want to emphasize, by example, that this account of music alone surfaces more or less perennially. It is not by any means the phlogiston of musical philosophy, although, of course, contemporary variants are not merely repetitions of the same old thing (any more than Schopenhauer was of Reid, or Reid of Hutcheson) but attempts to use the

8. Ibid., 1:256.

principle of representation in music while avoiding the weaknesses of preceding attempts. Let me instance two cases in point.

A casual look at what Hutcheson, Reid, and Schopenhauer say about representation in music alone is enough to reveal one glaring difficulty. It is fair to assume that, at least within reasonable limits, a normal "observer" will see in a convincing way *what* it is that a representation represents: what the object of representation is. Certainly this is true for representational painting. And even if, as is sometimes the case, one needs "prompting" by a text or title, as in representational music such as Vivaldi's *Seasons* or Bach's *Passions,* or prompting from a critic, as in the case of Erwin Panofsky's readings of painterly iconology, one gets the idea afterward, in some fairly convincing way; one sees it at last—or else rejects the representational interpretation. But none of this seems to be true in the examples of musical representation we have looked at so far. The suggested objects of representation range from the unconvincing to the impossible, from the merely quaint to the metaphysically bizarre. Certainly no one would find it transparent, in listening to Beethoven's C♯-Minor Quartet, that the music represents the human voice in a passion, or amiable conversation, or the thing-in-itself as striving will, as it would be transparent to the normal observer that a painting represents shoes, or flowers, or a woman holding a baby. Nor, I think, would one become convinced of it, and come to hear the work in one of those ways, after reading Hutcheson, or Reid, or Schopenhauer (or worse). I am not, by the way, denying that music bears some perceptible analogy to human expression. Indeed, I have argued elsewhere that it does, and that such philosophers as Hutcheson, Reid, and Schopenhauer (in his nonmetaphysical moments) were correct in arguing that this analogy accounts, in part, for many of the expressive qualities music may have.[9] But maintaining that position is very far indeed from maintaining that music alone is a repre-

9. On this see Peter Kivy, *The Corded Shell: Reflections on Musical Expression* (Princeton, N.J., 1980).

sentational art, and that the objects of its representation are voices, or conversations, or metaphysical reality, which amounts to saying these are its subjects or, even more implausibly, what it is "about," what it "reveals."

Recent tillers of the representational soil seem to be well aware of this difficulty, and what they have to say about pure music as a representational art is carefully stated in terms obviously calculated to avoid it. Richard Kuhns, in a recent note, presents what might be called a theory of pure music as "reflexive" representation. That is to say, following some well-known reflections of Arthur Danto's, mainly in regard to painting, Kuhns suggests that what we should think of as the "object" of representation in music alone is the music itself: music alone, in other words, is a self-representational or self-referential art. Thus: "Tones in music represent other tones. A modulation from major to minor refers as it moves, and establishes referring relationships as it sounds. . . . A harmonic tone refers to the prime tone; a prime tone refers to its harmonics. Tones both sound and refer as they sound. This mode of representation is one of music's most powerful representational capacities." Further: "Music is built on repetitions, repeats, themes and variations, modulations, twelve tone rows—all of these means are representational because each heard phrase or section leads the listener to hear other phrases and sections." And if it is a necessary condition of representation that medium of representation be distinguishable from its subject, then, Kuhns argues, musical self-representation fulfills that condition. "In all these cases listed above the hearer can distinguish the subject from the medium in the sense that he distinguishes each part, and the antecedent or simultaneous or anticipatory part, that it represents."[10] We can, then, accept, if we follow Kuhns here, that music alone is at least in part a representational art without having to accept such questionable, not to say downright implausible, objects of its rep-

10. Richard Kuhns, "Music as a Representational Art," *British Journal of Aesthetics* 18 (1978), 122.

resentation as voices, conversation, or the metaphysical will. The *music* is there; on that we all agree. If that is so, then the object of musical representation is, ipso facto, there as well; for it is that very same music.

I suspect that similar considerations are at the back of another recent attempt to "representationalize" pure instrumental music: that is to say, to have representation do the business without committing oneself to objects of representation that are at least unconvincing and at worst impossible. Jacques Barzun, long a defender of Berlioz's unquestionably programmatic works, wants to claim, as part of that defense, that "all music is programmatic, explicitly or implicitly, in more than one way." His reason for trying to defend this view, aside from wanting to make Berlioz look less singular, is much like Schopenhauer's reason for defending his own version of the representational theory: it appears to Barzun, as to Schopenhauer, to be the only way to explain the profound satisfaction that we take in "pure" (so-called) instrumental music. Barzun, unfortunately, I think, takes the view that music alone is truly contentless to imply that music alone must somehow be alien and remote from human life (in some sense or other that I, frankly, fail to understand) rather than assume it as a given to be explained that we *do* take profound pleasure in the contentless sound of "pure" (*properly* so-called) instrumental music. He argues: "It would be strange indeed if the arts, were they divorced from the actualities of human life, could exert the hold they do on both naive and sophisticated sensibilities. The mystery of music's power; the attribution of profundity, moral value, psychological penetration to its masterpieces; the incorrigible habit of saying what they 'really' mean . . .—all these common realities compel us to acknowledge that music is in its own inarticulate way an extension of human experience."[11]

Two key words here are "implicit" and "inarticulate." Of

11. Jacques Barzun, "The Meaning of Meaning in Music: Berlioz Once More," *Musical Quarterly* 66 (1980), 3, 16.

course the program of Berlioz's *Symphonie fantastique* or Kuhnau's "Biblical" Sonatas is there for all to see—no argument about that. But where is the program of Beethoven's C♯-Minor Quartet or Bach's *Inventions?* Clearly not out front—so, therefore, "implicit": it is the program beneath the surface, like Hutcheson's, Reid's, and Schopenhauer's deep representation. Barzun calls it "the hidden program." But what *is* the "hidden program" of Beethoven's Op. 131 or Bach's keyboard works? Any attempt to state it will, needless to say, be greeted with scorn, ridicule, and incredulity; and Barzun is far too musically sophisticated to fall into such a trap. So he must resort to the well-worn claim of ineffability. There is a program there, alright, but of course it cannot be expressed in mere words: it is an "inarticulate" program as befits music, the inarticulate art. Either that, or the program just is the music; that is, the musical course of the work, its form—in which case Barzun is saying much the same thing as Kuhns only in literary rather than pictorial terms: "program" instead of "representation." Thus Bach's Chaconne for unaccompanied violin, Barzun assures us, has a "program": "The 'program' is forever hidden in the mind [of Bach] that can thus communicate, but it exists." All works, however, to the extent they follow preexistent musical forms, have programs as well: so "the set forms of music each supply a program that the traditionally trained composer may elect by itself," in which case, even if we do not buy the "ineffable," hidden program of (say) Bach's Chaconne, we still must admit that it has a program and, indeed, one that can be stated merely by stating what a chaconne is and how Bach's instantiates it. Indeed, to cover all possible exigencies (at the cost of vacuity), Barzun has defined "program" so broadly that, on his definition, one can hardly think of anything that doesn't have one. "To cover all cases, it seems necessary to define as programmatic any scheme or idea, general or particular, that helps to determine the course of composition."[12]

12. Ibid., pp. 12, 5, 3.

For the better part of three centuries, then, which is to say, for nearly as long as we have had the modern institution of pure instrumental music, philosophers have attempted to put content into what seems to be contentless; representation into what seems to be pure abstraction; plot into inarticulate sound. What are we to make of these attempts?

The earlier ones are refreshingly falsifiable in fairly straight-forward and obvious ways, because the objects of representation that are involved—the human voice or human conversation—are so patently inadequate. Putting aside the other difficulties of representational accounts (which I will get to in a moment), it is clearly impossible, given the variety and complexity of instrumental forms already flourishing in the eighteenth century, to see them all as bearing enough analogy to human speech or conversation to be plausibly thought of as representations of them or to owe their effect to such a representational relation. But when we get to objects like the pure striving will as thing-in-itself, who can say? If there is such an entity, we are in no position to tell, in the ordinary way, whether or not music accurately represents it, or represents it at all, since it is not, as Kant would say, an object of possible experience for us or, in the plainer language of Berkeley, which for the occasion I appropriate from his argument against the representational theory of perception, the theory that "the ideas we perceive by our senses are not real things, but images or copies of them": "But as these supposed originals are in themselves unknown, it is impossible to know how far our ideas resemble them, or whether they resemble them at all."[13] The inaccessibility, in principle, of Schopenhauer's object of representation makes the claim of music to represent it immune from the usual kind of refutation based on an observed disanalogy between object and its depiction.

Of course, if, as most of us would doubtless agree, there is no such entity as Schopenhauer's metaphysical will, music can

13. George Berkeley, *Three Dialogues between Hylas and Philonous* (Indianapolis, Ind., 1954), p. 94 (third dialogue).

represent it only as pure intentional object, the tapestry to the unicorn, in which case we must accept some description of the metaphysical will against which to measure representational success. And in doing so we deprive the theory of its prima facie irrefutability. If we accept Schopenhauer's description— and whose else is there?—then it may be that certain passages in Franck's D-Minor Symphony (say), or the Prelude to *Tristan und Isolde,* seethe and bubble in the way that Schopenhauer's murky thing-in-itself might be imagined to do. But consider Joseph Haydn's Symphony No. 104. If you will not grant outright that it is a clear counterexample to the view that all music is a copy of the striving will, you must at least accept that, as a representation of Schopenhauer's meta-physical colossus, it is a colossal failure. Yet as a piece of pure instrumental music, it is one of the monuments. How can it be a representational failure, and yet its signal success as music alone be accounted for through its representational qualities?

With Kuhns and Barzun we come to conceptions of the object of musical representation that are, in the most obvious way, unfalsifiable by comparison of representation to object. For on Kuhns's view, the object of representation just is the medium of representation; and I take it that the relation of identity between object and depiction renders the question whether the purported depictions bears *enough* resemblance to its object to pass muster either nonsensical or trivially "yes." And on Barzun's view, when it does not come down to Kuhns's, the claim that pure instrumental music accurately portrays its "hidden program" remains in principle unverifia-ble because the hidden program is forever hidden, its content not verbalizable, and whereof one cannot speak. . . .

In any case, it would be philosophically unsound, even in circumstances where we can ask ourselves whether the pur-ported object of musical representation is a plausible one or not, to let the refutation of representationalism turn on that question. For there is no end of objects that the fertile imagina-tion can conjure up for music to represent. And it seems misguided to think that we must reject each new candidate for object of musical representation, *in infinitum,* before finally disposing of the view that music alone owes its effect to its "hidden" content, representationality, or program. Surely the view is unacceptable on more general grounds that would cover any and all purported objects. Do we not want to say here, as elsewhere, that everything is what it is and not another thing: that representational music represents and music alone does not, and that that is a basic datum of our experience which any account of music must accept?

Now, insisting that our enjoyment of pure, contentless music is a datum to be explained should not, I think, at least at the present stage of the argument, be suspected of begging the question at issue. I am not saying that simply because there is a contrast in ordinary musical usage between pure, contentless music and representational music, there may not be a way of explaining what perhaps merely appears contentless in terms of some hidden representational mechanism. But the burden of proof, if there is such a thing, is surely on the representationalist to show that, appearances to the contrary notwithstanding, there is a hidden or subliminal content to what we ordinarily call contentless music and what we ordinarily contrast with music that possesses an obvious and obviously intended representational content or narrative structure. Indeed, all too often the representationalist begs the question, insisting that so-called contentless music *must* have a representational content, in spite of the appearances, because it is the only possible explanation for our enjoyment and the only possible way of doing justice to the depth and importance of the purely musical experience. There is no clearer begging of the question than that. I do not say that a representational account of nonrepresentational music can be ruled out, a priori, simply because we call the music "nonrepresentational." I do say that the *at least* apparent nonrepresentationality of music is a datum that must be taken seriously: it is to be explained, not immediately to be explained away. And we need better reasons for a representational account than *merely* its familiarity, and the lame excuse that no other explanation comes readily to mind, to accept the reduction of so strong an impression of enjoyment in the contentless and abstract to something as clearly alien as enjoyment in representation.

For the moment, let me set aside Kuhns's suggestion that music represents itself and those of Barzun's remarks which seem very like it. This is a limiting or special case of representation, if a case at all, and requires separate treatment.

We are interested, then, in evaluating claims to the effect that pure, contentless instrumental music really is not pure and contentless but, rather, has a deep layer of representational qualities beneath its apparently abstract surface. Never mind what is represented—here the claims vary. We are now interested in evaluating these claims in their general form, ignoring the particular problems that their various proposed objects of representation might raise. The rest of the story is this. We require the representational account, it is claimed, to explain our appreciation of music alone; for that appreciation is like our appreciation of the other, representational arts; and our appreciation of *those* arts clearly lies in our appreciation of their representationality (as if the pleasure we take in representation were not itself mysterious and in need of an accounting; but I suppose one mystery is better than two, so let that pass).

Well, let us look more closely at the explanatory power of the representation theory as it applies to our appreciation of (the pleasure or satisfaction we take in) pure, contentless music. Suppose I am looking at a painting by van Gogh of a vase of flowers. I am, of course, fully aware of what is represented; if I were not, the satisfaction I take in various of the painting's representational aspects would clearly be denied me. I would not be able to enjoy, in other words, how the flowers were rendered. A creature form Alpha Centauri, where no flowers grow, could not enjoy van Gogh's painting as a representation.

But on the representational account of music alone, we are

all from Alpha Centauri, because we are not aware of the representational qualities in the deep layer that the music is supposed to have. This is implicit in the theory; for it is clear that the kind of musical representation we are talking about is not transparent to the listener but must be "discovered" by philosophy. That being the case, the explanatory power of the representational theory evaporates. For the pleasure we take in van Gogh's representation of the flowers is in seeing how the flowers are rendered, beginning at the most naive level of appreciation and going all the way to the painter's or critic's or art historian's appreciation of all of the painterly and expressive techniques employed. The whole explanatory power of representation as a source of pleasure derives from our perceiving the representation. Representation unperceived gives no satisfaction at all.

Nor is it plausible to argue that once philosophy reveals the representationality of "contentless" music, the representation can then function at the conscious level to provide the kind of satisfaction that van Gogh's painting does. For the listener has been getting deep satisfaction, no less than the connoisseur's pleasure in van Gogh, *prior* to having the representationality of the music "revealed." Indeed, that deep satisfaction is just what the representational theory is supposed to be needed to explain. The only avenue left open for the propounder of the representational theory is the appeal to an "unconscious" appreciation of musical representation, as Schopenhauer had already done. But such a move is deeply problematic. For if the representational theory of pure music was supposed to solve a mystery by appeal to the plain facts of pleasure in representationality, those plain facts are far behind us now, and we are faced with a mystery even more profound than why we take pleasure in pure, contentless musical abstraction: namely, why we take pleasure in representation of which we are not consciously aware. The point of reducing pure music to music with "content" is to make use of the plain fact that we enjoy representation when we consciously perceive it to explain our pleasure in pure music. Once we let go of this plain fact, we no longer have an explanation, and representation ceases to promise one.

I must hasten to add that I by no means rule out, in music or anywhere else, the plausibility of explanations in terms of unconscious perceptions or thoughts. I dare say the Freudian psychology of the unconscious has had little if anything to say about music alone to raise much hope in that direction. But Freud is by no means the only game in town. Recent experimental psychology has made use, with perfect empirical propriety, of appeals to unconscious visual thinking, for example, to explain experimental data, appeals that are surely not to be despised merely because they are appeals to *unconscious* perceptions.[14]

My criticism, rather, is directed against a specific case: the explanation of our enjoyment of music alone in terms of our unconsciously perceiving hidden representations. We have already seen the strategy here. The reason for our enjoyment of pure, apparently contentless music seems mysterious. Our enjoyment of representational art is a familiar pleasure and seems to some, perhaps, unmysterious and transparently obvious. But the problem is that if it is obvious why we enjoy representations, it is obvious only why we enjoy them *consciously*. At least, when one tries to understand our enjoyment of them, one does so in terms of conscious perception. As a matter of fact, it is, as I have suggested, not obvious at all why we enjoy consciously perceiving that an art work represents some subject matter or other. Aristotle tried to explain this enjoyment in terms of the pleasure he thought we all take in finding things out, that is to say, in learning. As Aristotle put it, in a very familiar passage near the beginning of the *Poetics,* "learning is most pleasant, not only for philosophers but for others likewise. . . . For this reason they delight in seeing images, because it comes about that they learn as they observe, and

14. I owe this example to Kendall Walton.

infer what each thing is."[15] I am sufficiently pessimistic about the state of the art to think that no one has come up with a better explanation than Aristotle's (which is not to say his is correct). But that is not the issue. The important point is that explanations like this one rely on enjoyment of some conscious response: in the case of Aristotle, I suppose, something like an "Ah! Ha!" phenomenon, a reaction of the kind "So that's the way it is!" or something like that.

But as soon as the representationalist is forced, as he or she must be in the case of music alone, to appeal to unconscious perception of representations, whatever, initial explanatory power and attraction the representational account may seem to have evaporates. For if we have at least some vague notion, Aristotle's or some other, of why it is pleasurable—as we know by direct acquaintance it is—to perceive artistic representations, we have no idea at all, I suggest, *why* it is or even *if* it is pleasurable to unconsciously perceive representations. Thus the representationalist's argument comes down to claiming that pure music *may* have hidden representations, we *may* unconsciously perceive them, and the unconscious perception of hidden representations *may,* we know not how or why, be pleasurable. Such an argument is not much to get excited about. And the reason why representational accounts like Barzun's tend to carry conviction is, I think, that we are never really brought to the hard realization that we are dealing with something far different from the ordinary perception of representation with its obvious pleasurable concomitant, well-known if not well-understood.

Thus I do not say an explanation of our enjoyment in music alone in terms of unconsciously perceived representations is *impossible.* I say that, at the present time, it is implausible, or at least without positive evidence in its favor, and gains whatever

15. Aristotle, *Poetics,* with the *Tractatus Coislinianus,* reconstruction of *Poetics* II, and the fragments of the *On Poets,* trans. Richard Janko (Indianapolis, Ind., 1987), p. 4 (48b).

attraction it may have by sloppily trading on what it is not entitled to: the *obvious* explanatory power of our *consciously* perceiving representations and the familiar enjoyment we take in that. The notion that we consciously perceive representations in pure music is patently false. The notion that we unconsciously perceive them is possible but unsupported and, as an explanatory hypothesis of our musical pleasure, unhelpful into the bargain.

Surely, though, we *can* hear pure music representationally. Helen does: she hears heroes and shipwrecks in Beethoven's Fifth. That is so, and there are a number of replies one might make.

One might reply that although we can listen to pure music this way, we shouldn't; it is not the best way to listen. I believe that statement is true, but it requires an argument, and I do not wish to give that argument here.

One might reply that if we are talking about what is *in* pure music for us to hear and appreciate, what Helen is doing is beside the point. She is "free associating" to music; we can all do that. But what she "hears" is not in the music and therefore has nothing to do with whether that music is representational. There are no heroes or shipwrecks in it. I believe that statement is also true, but it too requires an argument, and I do not want to give that argument here.

I want simply to reply with what requires no argument at all. Some do, indeed, listen to pure music the way Helen does, heroes, shipwrecks, and all. But some, like Margaret, hear only music; and some, like Tibby, follow the score—no heroes or shipwrecks for them. They too get deep satisfaction from music, and, quite simply, it is my purpose here to talk about them. That is all. Forget about whether Margaret's or Tibby's way is the better way. It is a *way,* and it requires an accounting.

But there is, we must now recall, a version of the representational account that needs neither heroes nor shipwrecks, for it claims only that music represents itself. On that view, there is no conflict between the assertion that music represents and the assertion that Margaret hears only music, for the content of the representation *is* only the music. How, then, are we to respond?

Let me adduce three examples, so that we will have something specific to talk about: they fall under the categories of "representation," "narration," and "meaning." Kuhns tells us that tones represent other tones in that they refer to them, either backward or forward in musical time; that is, a certain chord, a dominant seventh (say), may lead me to expect the tonic and so "represents" what is to come; or there may occur a certain phrase that is a variation of a previously heard phrase and so "represents" what has happened before. Barzun tells us that a piece of music written in a certain musical form has a "program," namely, that form. So, for example, the first movement of Haydn's Symphony No. 104 is in monothematic sonata form: the story it narrates is *that*. Finally, Leonard Meyer, in his highly influential book *Emotion and Meaning in Music,* understands "meaning" in such a way (derived from information theory) that, to put it baldly, music means itself. "That is, one musical event (be it a tone, a phrase, or a whole section) has meaning because it points to and makes us expect another musical event."[16]

Now one way, and a perfectly harmless way, of understanding each of these claims is as a *façon de parler,* more or less illuminating as the case may be. Never mind that "represent," "program," and "mean" may not be being used in their standard senses. They are, let us say, revealing metaphors: they help to show us some of the pure musical properties that music alone possesses and that we take pleasure in when we listen to it. With that way of looking at these claims I have no quarrel at all and gladly accept such descriptions as Kuhns, Barzun, and Meyer offer, in that light, as true descriptions of the pure musical parameters. In Meyer's case, indeed, that is clearly all

16. Leonard Meyer, *Emotion and Meaning in Music* (Chicago, 1956), p. 35.

that is meant; for, as he says, "This is what music means from the viewpoint of the absolutist."[17]

But there is also here a danger that we must carefully guard against. Since the emergence of pure instrumental music as a major musical enterprise, people have been asking questions like "What's it of?" "What's it about?" "What's it mean?" Behind the first question is a sense of "represent" that people get from such paradigms as van Gogh's representation of flowers, behind the second a sense of "narrative" that people get from such paradigms as Thomas Mann's story about a man who falls in love with a boy and dies in Venice, behind the third a sense of "meaning" that people get from the semantics of natural languages, where words can be defined, sentences paraphrased and translated. But Kuhn's sense of "represent" has only, as far as I can see, the necessary condition of reference in common with the paradigm, if even that (I don't think it is sufficient); Barzun's sense of "program," in which the program of a movement can be its form, conveys no sense at all of narrative; Meyer's sense of "meaning" is the sense in which clouds "mean" rain, not the sense in which "horse" means "equine quadruped" or "Arma virumque cano" means "Arms and the man I sing." They are all special senses, terms of art, or pared-down, abstracted senses. And there is nothing wrong in that, as long as one remembers it. What is a fallacy, something like what Whitehead called the "fallacy of misplaced concreteness," is to forget that, although Kuhns says pure instrumental music "represents," his answer to the presystematic question "What's it [a representation] of?" is, really, "Nothing," or to forget that although Barzun says pure instrumental music has "programs," his answer to the presystematic question "What's it about?" is, really, "Nothing," or to forget that although Meyer says pure instrumental music has "meaning" (or, rather, "means"), his answer to the presystematic question "What's it mean?" is, real-

17. Ibid.

ly, "Nothing." For the people who ask and have asked those questions mean and have meant by "represent," "program," and "mean" something else than what Kuhns, Barzun, and Meyer do; or, to be exact, something *more*.

Further, because these special, theoretical senses of "represent," "program," and "mean" do not have the content of their presystematic senses, they cannot be appealed to in any obvious way to explain the pleasure we take in pure instrumental music. That is, we cannot just say that since pure instrumental music "represents" (in Kuhns's sense), or "narrates," has a "program" (in Barzun's sense), or has "meaning" (in Meyer's sense), the pleasure we take in music alone can consequently be explained as the kind of pleasure we take in van Gogh's representation of a vase of flowers, or in Mann's narrative of love and death in Venice, or in the propositional meaning of a treatise on metaphysics. As the senses of "represent," "program," and "mean" are far from the presystematic senses, the plain facts of appreciation that those presystematic senses suggest cannot be simply assumed. They must be argued for. (It may be obvious why a representation by van Gogh of a vase of flowers give pleasure. It is hardly obvious why three quarter-notes in measure 43 should give pleasure, on the assumption that they "represent" three quarter-notes in measure 78.)

Finally, it is well to note that behind Kuhns's concept of musical representation lies an important theoretical consideration. His source, as Kuhns explicitly states, is the work of Arthur Danto. Now Danto, both in the early articles to which Kuhns refers and in his book *The Transfiguration of the Commonplace,* is engaged in an ambitious theoretical project, one of the purposes of which is to establish, as an essential property of art, its "aboutness."[18] That being the case, it is nontrivial for Danto that music "represent," which is to say, be "about," in

18. See Arthur C. Danto, *The Transfiguration of the Commonplace: A Philosophy of Art* (Cambridge, Mass., 1981).

some logically acceptable sense of these words. Of painting and the literary arts there is no question (at least in the central cases); but if the grand scheme is to go through, music too must be accorded the same logical status. For anyone with these theoretical commitments, then, it would seem that calling music "representational," and "about" itself, must go beyond the merely metaphorical. Whereas musical common sense dictates that it not go as far as the presystematic sense in which van Gogh "represented" a vase of flowers or Vivaldi the seasons. I have no such theoretical commitments myself; nor, however, do I have any real reason to think that someone who does is necessarily saying anything inconsistent with what I shall say here about music alone. Between the metaphorical and the presystematic there may well be logical space sufficient to accommodate a sense of music representing itself that can both fulfill Danto's theoretical requirements and yet avoid overrepresentationalizing pure, contentless instrumental music. That notion, however, is for those with such theoretical aspirations to work out. For my own part, I will have to wait and see whether what eventuates will be compatible with the views developed here.

I ended the previous chapter by remarking that the stimulation model, for all of its palpable inadequacies, did have one thing right. It is now time to say what that one thing is. Being a purely nonepistemic, causal theory of musical pleasure, the stimulation model leaves absolutely no place for musical "content." In that, and in that alone, it is profoundly and obviously correct. But the representational model has something right too, as we have seen, something that the stimulation model has profoundly and obviously incorrect. It construes music as an object of the understanding, not merely a stimulus to the nervous system.

It would seem that the thesis of musical stimulation and the antithesis of musical representation present us now, and historically, with a clear-cut dilemma. We seem to be able to have an account of music alone, the stimulation model, that does justice to its purity—but at the unacceptable cost of making it a mindless titillation. We seem to be able to have an account, the representational model, that does justice to its status as an object for the intellect—but at the unacceptable cost of imposing a content on it and belying its purity.

But surely this is a false dilemma. We can construe music alone as an object for the mind without at the same time having to construe it as a representational or propositional object, in order, as it were, to legitimate its intellectual pretensions. Music alone is of the mind and of the world. It is not about the world, or about anything else, except, perhaps, itself. Let us get down now to the task of spelling this out.

CHAPTER 5 /

Margaret's Way, Tibby's Way

There would seem to be a world of difference between the average person's experience of music and the experience (say) of Joseph Haydn when he first heard the string quartets Mozart dedicated to him; a world of difference between Mrs. Munt "mindlessly" beating her foot when the tunes come round and Tibby, profoundly versed in counterpoint, following the score on his knee. A quantitative world of difference indeed there is; but there is no qualitative difference at all.

It is tempting to imagine Haydn's experience as one full of thinking, thinking about how Mozart did this or that: the way in which a modulation was handled, the contrapuntal devices employed in a fugal passage, a new sonority exploited on the viola, and so forth. But Mrs. Munt, if she is thinking about anything whatever, is not thinking about the music. How can she be? How can one be thinking about something one has no knowledge of at all? Perhaps she is thinking about Tibby, or Margaret, or an appointment she has tomorrow. As far as the music goes, however, she is just responding to it as my knee responds to the doctor's little rubber hammer.

This may be a tempting way to look at things, but it is profoundly wrong. The difference between Mrs. Munt and

Tibby, between the average listener and Haydn, is not the difference between those who respond to music as a physical stimulus and those who respond to it as a cognized object. I lay it down as something of an axiom that those who respond to sound merely as a physical stimulus are not responding to music and that those like Mrs. Munt who obviously are responding to music are responding to a cognized object of attention. I will not defend the former claim; I cannot. I will defend the latter one by trying to show how, appearances to the contrary notwithstanding, Mrs. Munt and others like her are responding to a cognized object of attention and what that object is like.

From Mrs. Munt to Haydn, I am suggesting, there is a continuum of more and more complex cognition and, as I will try to show in the next chapter, more and more complex objects of cognition, even though the sounds (as physical stimuli) are the same, where Mrs. Munt, Tibby, and Haydn are listening to the same work. Common wisdom, then, would dictate that I begin with Mrs. Munt and, having explicated her perception of music, go on to Tibby and Haydn; for common wisdom has it, I presume, that we go from the simple to the complex. But there is good reason, in this particular instance, to reverse the usual procedure, and go from the complex to the simple. The reason is this. It should be obvious to everyone that when Haydn listens to Mozart's quartets, he is attending to a cognized, thought-about object. And it seems altogether clear what sort of object it is, what sort of thinking is going on. The object is what the abstract language of musical theory and analysis (as understood by Haydn) describes; the thinking is about that object, informed, in addition, by the composer's craft. It is Mrs. Munt who poses the problem. For it is not at all clear what object she is attending to (surely not the object described by theory and analysis, of which she knows nothing) or what musical thinking is going on in her head, empty, as it is, of musical knowledge. So we had better start with the obvious, with what Tibby and Haydn are thinking about it.

Only then will we undertake the task of trying to show that, even in Mrs. Munt's case, there is musical cognition and an object thereof. And we must show that there is such cognition, or we will be justly charged with examining only one kind of musical appreciation, the "intellectual" kind, while ignoring the "mindless" response of the average listener, by no means to be scorned. That there is only one kind of musical appreciation, and that it is never mindless, is the result we want; and the best way to get that result, it would seem, is to go from the obviously concept-laden listening of Tibby to the not-at-all obvious but, I believe, nevertheless concept-laden listening of Mrs. Munt, even though, in so doing, we reverse the order of common sense and the *Discourse on Method* and go from the more complex to the less.

I can think of no better way of proceeding—indeed, no other way—than to talk about myself: a Tibby somewhere between Margaret and Haydn. I will talk about my own experience of music, as it seems to me to be, and work my way from there to Mrs. Munt. (I presume it is not a problem to work my way from me to Haydn as, if it is obvious that my musical appreciation is concept-laden, it is even more obvious that Haydn's appreciation, orders of magnitude more informed than mine, is as well.)

Nor am I worried about generalizing from my own case alone; for although I am generalizing from a single case, I am not generalizing from a singular one. I share, with all others at my musical level, a common musical education and, because of that, a common approach to listening: common listening habits.

Let me add one other comment by way of preamble to my method here. There is, I think, solid theoretical grounding in philosophy of mind, philosophy of perception, psychology, and philosophical psychology for the assertion that the musical experience is, indeed must be, a cognitive one. I share that theoretical outlook with the contemporary practitioners of those disciplines. However, I come to the conclusions I do not because I have done my theoretical homework but rather because it seems to me to be what my own musical experience amounts to. I have come to my view empirically, with myself as the laboratory.

I begin with a familiar case from Kant's third *Critique*. Kant writes there of the beauty of bird songs: "[M]ost likely our sympathy with the mirth of a dear little creature is confused with the beauty of its song, for if exactly imitated by man (as has been sometimes done with the notes of the nightingale) it would strike our ear as wholly destitute of taste."[1] Kant's point is that we must be enjoying not the beauty of the sounds that the bird is making but the thought of the bird's happy disposition (or something of the kind), because those same sounds, when we know they are being produced by a human being, cease to seem beautiful to us. But a different construction might well be put on this example, to wit, that in enjoying the bird song I am indeed enjoying the beauty of sounds but under a certain description: "sounds of a bird." And those same sounds, under the description "sounds of a human bird imitator," might not produce the same (or any) pleasure. Now I am not suggesting that, in the two cases, we are hearing "different" sounds, because in the one case I enjoy them and in the other I do not (or not as much). I am not suggesting that the heard quality of the sounds must be different when the sounds are heard under the description "song of a bird" from what it is when they are heard under the description "sounds of a bird imitator." I don't know how to tell if that is true or not, and I am not even sure I know what it means. On the only "objective" test I can think of, one that filters out the pleasure factor—a reading on an oscilloscope (or some such instrument)—the sounds are the "same" in both instances. What I am suggesting is that enjoying the song of a bird is a case of taking pleasure in physical stimulation. Sounds are,

---

1. Immanuel Kant, *Critique of Aesthetic Judgement,* trans. James Creed Meredith (Oxford, 1911), p. 89.

after all, a physical stimulus. But the kind of enjoyment is very different from that pure stimulus-pleasure we must imagine a cat (say) gets by rubbing against your leg or the leg of a chair—it makes no difference to the cat, and that is a clue to the difference between the cat's pure stimulus-pleasure and my pleasure in the bird song. For I am taking pleasure in those sounds *as* sounds produced by a bird; I am enjoying the sounds under a description that has all kinds of reverberations in my belief system and in the cultural life I lead. My pleasure is "full of mind," a complex function of concepts, beliefs, emotions; and it makes all the difference in the world to my enjoyment whether I believe these sounds I am enjoying are produced by a nightingale or an Indian scout, even though it makes no difference at all to the oscilloscope.

Indeed, I would go so far as to conjecture that such cognitive elements are present in all the pleasure adult human beings take in physical stimulation, no matter how simple and primitive. Imagine that you are running your hand over the surface of what you take to be an eighteenth-century table, enjoying the wonderful smoothness of the surface. You then discover that it is not *echt* but a rather well-designed copy manufactured in Grand Rapids. You scarcely enjoy the smoothness of the surface as much, or at least you enjoy it in a different way, under the description "massproduced by machinery to close tolerances" as under the description "handplaned by skilled craftsman." The surface is the same, to be sure, and the stimulation it produces on the surface of your hand, and the nerves therein, doubtless the same as well. But the pleasure you take in the sensation, I submit, is quite different, in a completely uncontroversial sense. For example, the degree of smoothness will not be as impressive—it consequently will not be enjoyed as much—under the latter description as under the former; for the standard of smoothness relative to eighteenth-century craftsmanship will be lower than the standard relative to twentieth-century technology.

The point I am making here is simply that we enjoy sensual

experiences, even of the most direct and seemingly "mind-less" kind, as "experiences of. . . ." And the point holds for musical enjoyment too. Let me begin to make out that case by adducing an example, which I will call *Cherchez le thème.*

One of the things I do when I listen to a fugue, of course, is to listen for the entrances of the theme. Sometimes I get it right, sometimes I miss an entrance because it is in an "inner voice" or otherwise disguised, sometimes I am fooled into thinking there is an entrance when, in fact, it is only a scrap of the theme in an "episode." That is something I enjoy when I listen to fugues. I presume others enjoy it too.

Certainly, "finding the theme" is one of the musical enjoy-ments the fugue is meant to afford. Indeed, an earlier instru-mental form, somewhat fuguelike, the sixteenth- and seven-teenth-century ricercar, made it quite plain in its very name, which comes from the Italian *ricercare,* "to search." One of the pleasures we take in such imitative contrapuntal music as the ricercar and the fugue lies in the search: in the seeking and finding. But, needless to say, in order to seek and to find, the music must be an object of cognition for me. I must under-stand it under the description "fugue"; I must know what the "theme" is; I must be able to "perceive that" the theme has appeared; and "perceiving that" is a kind of "knowing" (or "believing") that. . . .

I shall now make so bold as to suggest that this special case of musical enjoyment can be generalized for *all* musical enjoy-ment. I realize that such a claim must seem to the reader utterly incredible. So what I shall now attempt to do is to anticipate some of the more obvious objections to this claim and proceed to answer them. In so doing, I will, at the same time, be explicating the claim and making it stick. Here, then, are some objections that, I imagine, will come immediately to mind. (Of course I cannot anticipate them all.)

Objection (1). You have stuffed the listener's head full of conscious thoughts, intentions, mind-sets that may indeed be present when Haydn listens to Mozart but could scarcely be present when Mrs. Munt listens to Beethoven. Mrs. Munt knows nothing of "themes," "episodes," "entrances," and the like. She doesn't know anything about music; she just knows what she likes. She likes Beethoven and taps her foot. But she cannot think about what she doesn't know anything about. Music may be for the experts, but it is also for all of the Mrs. Munts, who go to concerts to enjoy, not to think.

Objection (2). Forget about Mrs. Munt. Your account won't even work for your most favorable case: Haydn listening to Mozart. Granted, one particular stance that a very knowledgeable listener might take to music would be an "analytic" one. A composer might listen to another composer's work with an eye to analyzing the "craft of musical composition." But, of course, much of the true musical experience would be missed in so doing. Haydn may take the analytic stance toward Mozart's quartets, but he will be too busy analyzing them to enjoy them. The music goes round and round. We have no time to think about it while it passes by. If we tried, we would lose the thread. You can't think and listen to music at the same time. Enjoying music cannot be the conscious process you make it out to be, even in those cases where you could assume the listener capable of thinking about it. Thinking about music is one thing, enjoying it quite another. Music is a blessed release from thought.

Objection (3). It is utterly absurd to generalize from this case to all musical enjoyment. This is, indeed, a kind of musical enjoyment but, after all, a very special, intellectual enjoyment, as the fugue and ricercar are very special, intellectual forms of music that appeal to few concertgoers. (Remember the definition of a *fugue* that goes: "A piece of music where the voices enter one-by-one and the audience leaves one-by-one.") You can hardly explain, in a similar way, for example, the immense pleasure one takes in a Romantic melody such as the exquisite theme in the slow section of Tchaikovsky's *Francesca da Rimini* or, an even tougher because so much simpler instance, the pleasure one takes in "Greensleeves," played without any accompaniment on a recorder. That's also music, and music to far more people than a Bach fugue or a ricercar by Frescobaldi.

Objection (4). Let us suppose that some musical features are enjoyed in the way you say: in the process of perceiving *that* . . . . Nevertheless, there are some features of music we enjoy where such an explanation is simply a nonstarter. "Mozart was just three years old," we are told by his first biographer, "when his sister (then aged seven), had her first clavier lessons, and here the boy's genius first came to light. He would often sit at the clavier of his own accord and amuse himself for hours harmonising thirds, and when he found them he would play them and was greatly delighted."[2] Whether or not the story is worthy of belief, it is certainly believable. One can easily imagine a three-year-old of Mozart's genius being pleased by thirds. But his tender age points up the fact that this is a pure, "mindless" musical pleasure. What, after all, did Mozart know about thirds at the age of three? Even Mozart had his limits, although I dare say his father would have told the world, if the old boy could have gotten away with it, that Wolfgang sang rather than cried when the midwife smacked his bottom. Nor need we, in making the point, rely on such an exotic example. To hear the glorious sound Arthur Grumiaux achieves by simply drawing his bow across the G-string is to experience a pure musical pleasure. And pure musical pleasure is also experienced merely in hearing a C-major chord. Such minimal musical events provide, perhaps, minimal musical pleasure. But *musical pleasure* they *do* provide. They provide it to adults, to be sure, who may be full of musical knowledge, unlike little Wolferl, striking thirds on the clavier at the age of three. That knowledge, however, avails us nothing in trying to explain the pleasure adults take in these minimal musical events. Where is there

2. Franz Niemetschek, *Life of Mozart,* trans. Helen Mautner (London, 1956), p. 13.

knowledge here? What need I know to experience the pure sensuous beauty of pure instrumental tone or harmonic quality? Surely what we have here are pure stimulus pleasures, yet *musical* pleasures. Here, then, is an exception that disproves the rule.

Objection (5). The question, of course, is certain to arise in the reader's mind why we take pleasure in finding the theme and in other related perceptual activities of musical listening. That is to say, if this is meant to be an account of why music alone is enjoyed, it remains incomplete, indeed vacuous, if I fail to suggest just what it is about the central activities of musical listening that should make them enjoyable.

Objection (6). Music offers a myriad, a plethora of features, and it is clearly not possible that one example of musical enjoyment, such as has been adduced in this little discussion of fugue and ricercar, could possibly account for our enjoyment of them all. Least of all would it be possible to *prove* that the example of musical perception and enjoyment adduced above—or rather, the type of musical perception and enjoyment of which it is a token—can serve as an explanatory model for all of the pleasures we take in music alone. Granted, present ingenuity may have exhausted temporarily the supply of counterexamples; the hypothesis may *seem* secure. But until it be established beyond reasonable doubt that there are no possible counterexamples, it would be ill-advised, given our intuition about the inexhaustibility of kinds of pure musical pleasure, to adopt the proposed hypothesis. And to establish such a thing beyond a reasonable doubt is clearly not possible.

Such, I imagine, are some of the objections that might be brought against accepting the suggestion I have made about pure musical enjoyment. Let us see now how they might be answered. To do so, I want first to expatiate a bit more on my example.

I said, it will be recalled, that one of the musical pleasures the fugue and ricercar afford us is the pleasure of seeking and finding the statements of the theme. It would be more accurate to say that the pleasure is a complex one, lying in our perception *that* the theme has entered and in *how* the theme enters where we find it. That is to say, the pleasure does not lie just in my finding the theme. If that were the case, I would get as much musical pleasure from a fugue by Telemann as from one by Bach. To put it vaguely, at first, I take pleasure in *how* the theme enters; and *how* I hear it entering is a function of how much I know about and can perceive in fugues. In the final analysis, let me add, what I enjoy, broadly speaking, is how *beautifully* the theme enters, the description of what it is that I find beautiful being relative to what I know, the pleasure taken being relative to just how beautiful I find it to be. (And if someone should ask me to define musical beauty, I would, of course, decline the invitation, as any sensible person ought.)

I might, for example, take pleasure in the way the theme enters, quite unexpectedly, on a degree of the scale other than the usual one, thus giving it a different harmonic cast, even though the intervals and rhythm are enough alike to make it a clearly recognizable instance. Or I might take pleasure in how it enters before a previous statement has finished, that is, in a stretto.

What must be noted here is that there are various descriptions under which I might put my pleasurable experience. I might say, if asked, "I enjoyed the funny way the theme sounded just then, when it came in: like the way it sounded before, but somehow a little different; I don't know, maybe a little more somber." Or I might say, "I enjoyed how Bach sneaked that theme in, starting on the seventh degree of the scale rather than the first; and, of course, in doing that he gave the theme a whole new harmonic structure and cast." I might say, "I enjoyed the way everything sort of gets crowded at that spot, as if everyone is trying to rush through a narrow doorway at once." Or I might say, "I enjoyed particularly the way Bach handled the stretto; I didn't realize, when I first heard the theme in the beginning, that such a complex theme could possibly combine with itself four times, only two beats apart—each time I listen to that stretto, it amazes me." Now in both the former instances one is perceiving the "same" musical event but under different descriptions; and that is so of the latter two instances as well.

What I first want to draw attention to is the wide range of musical auditors who might enjoy even so "intellectual" a musical form as the fugue. One can take pleasure in a stretto for many of the right reasons without understanding it under the description "stretto" (with all that word implies); *but,* and this is the point to be underscored, one must understand it under *some* appropriate description or other to appreciate it at all. Indeed, that is my claim: that when someone is enjoying music, he or she is, in any given instance, enjoying some sonic quality of a piece of music perceived under a certain description as doing something the listener enjoys, as doing something beautifully.

With this in mind we can turn to Objection (1) and conclude, directly, that it has no merit at all. To be sure, Mrs. Munt cannot enjoy the entrance of a fugue subject under the description "a disguised entrance on the seventh degree of the scale" or the overlapping of entrances as "an ingeniously managed stretto with the voices entering two beats apart." She possesses neither those concepts nor, consequently, those thoughts. But she can enjoy the way a theme appears, and she can enjoy a stretto. She just does not enjoy them under music-theoretical descriptions. Indeed, it is clear that Mrs. Munt does enjoy the entrance of themes, because, as you can see, she beats her foot contentedly when they come around in Beethoven's Fifth. And she must perceive *that* they have come around—hence *know* that they have come around—or she would not enjoy that aspect of the symphony which, clearly, she does enjoy. If you asked her, "What did you enjoy just now in the symphony," she would not, of course, answer: "The way Beethoven brought back the second subject in the tonic key in the recapitulation." She does not possess the concepts "tonic," "second subject," and "recapitulation." But she does possess *some* concepts under which she perceives and enjoys the return of themes, or, I submit, she would not be able to perceive the return of themes and enjoy the symphony at all. (How or whether ants or cats or spiders "perceive," human beings' perceptions are concept-laden). If you ask Mrs. Munt what she enjoys just now, in the symphony, when she starts beating her foot, perhaps she will say: "I love that place where that other tune, not the one in the beginning, comes back again, sort of different, comfortably—like coming home to tea." If you think that is banal enough for Mrs. Munt, then let it stand for what she "hears"; if you think it is too clever, doubtless you will be able to come up with the appropriate level of banality. But the point is, there exists some level appropriate to any enjoyer of that particular aspect of Beethoven's Fifth Symphony. We needn't stuff every listener's head with thoughts at the level of Joseph Haydn's to insist that some musical thinking must be going on in any case of musical enjoyment.

But this brings us right up against Objection (2). For it now appears that, on my view, Mrs. Munt's head is as full of musical thoughts, while listening to music, as Haydn's is. But surely that is not possible. The experience of music is a "spontaneous" flow. How can all of these thoughts about music, whether the technical ones of Haydn or the banal, commonplace ones of Mrs. Munt, possibly keep up with what is passing by? Why, we should be so preoccupied with thinking about the music that we would not have attention left to listen to it, like the senator who was so busy defending the Constitution that he never had time to read it.

This, however, is clearly both to underestimate our mental and perceptual capacities and to misconstrue consciousness into the bargain. Let me begin, though, by acknowledging that no listener, short of a Mozart-like intellect, ever does pay full attention to the music. I cannot honestly say that my mind does not wander, at times, and become distracted by "alien"

thoughts, or even thoughts about the music leading me away
from it, so that I find myself at the recapitulation without quite
knowing how I got there from the double bar. It would be
foolish to deny that thinking, even thinking about the music,
sometimes does get in the way of musical attention. The question is, does thinking about the music one is listening to of
necessity get in the way of listening to (and enjoying) it? And
it seems to me, when we properly understand the situation,
that the answer is "no."

First of all, it is simply to underestimate the capacities of
human thought and perception to suggest that I cannot think
about what I am perceiving and perceive, at the same time,
activities that, by the way, can be talked about as separate but
that in actuality are inextricably intertwined. An analogy may
make this point more obvious. Suppose that I am completely
absorbed in putting together an intricate piece of machinery—
(say) a clock. I am, of course, perceiving the bits and pieces of
the clock with some care; and I am, all the while, thinking
about what I am doing; if I weren't, I would surely make a
mess of it. Finally, I am also engaged in the activity of putting
the pieces together. I am perceiving, doing, and thinking
about what I am perceiving and doing, all at the same time.
No one would deny that human beings have the capacity to do
all of those things at once when putting together a clock. And
it is claiming no more—perhaps less—to assert that Mrs.
Munt can perceive the music and think about it, in her fashion,
at the same time. One needn't be Mozart to do that; one need
only be human.

But perhaps the skeptical will not be satisfied to let the
argument rest here. I imagine the following rejoinder might
well be forthcoming: "Surely you are not suggesting that,
while listening to Beethoven's Fifth, Mrs. Munt is *consciously*
thinking things like, Well, there is that old tune again, coming
comfortably home to tea, or anything like that. Just *ask* Mrs.
Munt what she was conscious of thinking while listening to
the symphony, and I wager she will not be able to come up

with anything. If that doesn't prove to you that Mrs. Munt's enjoyment of music has nothing to do with her consciously thinking about it, I don't know what will."

This sounds convincing, but I think it is the result of a deep confusion. Of course it might well be that Mrs. Munt does not remember what or that she was thinking about the music while listening to Beethoven's Fifth, and that possibility must always be taken into account. It would hardly be plausible, though, to claim that it is always so: such a claim sounds like protecting a favored theory simply by making it immune to falsification. There is, however, a much more plausible response. What the skeptic fails to distinguish here is the difference between thinking, *consciously,* about the music and being *conscious* of one's thinking, that is to say, being aware and perceiving that (and what) one is thinking. In the former case it is the music that is the object of one's thoughts; in the latter case it is one's thinking that is the object. The skeptic is confusing the two or, rather, taking the latter as a necessary condition for the former. That is to say, the skeptic thinks that if Mrs. Munt is consciously thinking about the music when she is listening to Beethoven's Fifth, she must be consciously aware *that* she is thinking about the music, must also have her thoughts about Beethoven's Fifth as objects of her thinking. That claim is plainly false. I ascribe to Mrs. Munt conscious thoughts about the music, not conscious thoughts about her conscious thoughts (about the music). And it is because the common run of listeners, like Mrs. Munt, do not think about their thinking, are not attending to their thoughts, that they cannot tell you that, or a fortiori what, they are thinking when they listen to music.

I am not, by the way, denying that one can both think about the music (in listening to it) and think about what one is thinking at the same time. Such a denial would again be to underestimate human cognitive and perceptual capacities. I think about music and think about my thinking, while listening to it, a great deal of the time these days. But that, of course, is because I am engaged in writing this book and am committed, as a result, to an analysis of my thoughts about music. Few people who listen to music have that end in view: certainly not the Mrs. Munts, and seldom the Tibbys or Haydns, either. However, to repeat my point: to think consciously about music (or anything else) is not to be conscious of one's thinking; and it is only conscious thinking, not consciousness of thinking, that I ascribe to the musical listener. If one bears this distinction in mind, then Objection (2) should hold no terrors at all.

The import of Objection (3) is twofold: there is the general caveat that we cannot take the musical pleasures of so intellectual a form as the fugue as an explanatory model for the many nonintellectual pleasures that music affords; and—a special case—we certainly cannot take the "problem-solving" pleasure afforded by such things as finding the fugue theme as an explanatory model for that most direct, spontaneous, unintellectual pleasure we take in what for most people is not merely an important musical parameter but almost music itself: namely, melody.

Whatever truth there is in the notion that the fugue is a cerebral art form need not trouble us. For many of the "intellectual" pleasures the fugue affords are not by any means restricted to the fugue; and although they may be more abundant there, they are sufficiently abundant in "low" as well as "high" forms of less learned music to account for a great deal of our musical enjoyment in those other forms. Indeed, we have already noticed that *Cherchez le thème* is the game Mrs. Munt is playing when her foot starts to tap as the tunes appear and reappear in Beethoven's Fifth. And it is surely the game we play when we listen to all of the various kinds of jazz that involve variations on popular songs.

But all of these instances involve, of course, what we perceive in the "structure" of music. What about the melody that, as so many think and have thought, is the part of music that goes directly to the heart and the senses—as many in the eighteenth century saw it, that part which is the soul, the inspiration, the expression of music rather than the craft or the learning? What about that? What about "Greensleeves"?

Well, as an antidote to such thinking about melody, let us remind ourselves that a melody, like a fugue or a symphony, is not a musical monad but a musical structure; and far from being transparent to perception, it frequently costs us much labor to fully appreciate, as it cost its composer, far more frequently than is thought, much labor to create.

Consider, by way of example, the slow theme from *Francesca da Rimini,* mentioned in Objection (3). The program annotator writes, on the record sleeve of one recording, "The theme that represents the girl is one of the most beautiful Tchaikovsky ever composed; with scarcely a pause for breath it unwinds over more than thirty bars."[3] If one were to listen to that theme for the first time, with the expectation of hearing "one of the most beautiful Tchaikovsky ever wrote" (which, given the comparison class, is very high praise), one would, I think, be initially disappointed. For the theme starts on something of a cliché, echoing a well-worn eighteenth-century formula (see Examples 1 and 2). It is only in the third measure that the thing begins to soar, and one gradually begins to see the Romantic implications of its "unwinding." My point is that the theme is not immediately appealing; that it has a structure which must be perceived before it will yield up its melodic beauty and (thus) afford musical satisfaction; that, in other words, this paradigm of melodic invention from one of the most popular composers in the classical canon, admired above all for his lyric gifts, is far from the spontaneous gush, transparent to perception, that bypasses the mind of a direct line to the heart. To enjoy this melody is to enjoy that, as the annotator says, it "unwinds" with "scarcely a pause for breath," that it transforms itself in our perceptual experience from a

3. Andrew Clements, on the record sleeve of the London recording by the Cleveland Orchestra under the direction of Riccardo Chailly.

Example 1. Peter Ilyich Tchaikovsky, *Francesca da Rimini,* Op. 32

Example 2. Georg Friedrich Handel, Sonata in B Minor for Flute and Continuo, Op. 1, No. 9

cliché seemingly leading nowhere to a line of almost limitless expanse, and so on. The enjoyment of this melody is thought-laden, as is the enjoyment of a stretto or augmentation in a fugue.

To be sure, and almost needless to say at this point, Mrs. Munt may not enjoy the convolutions of the *Francesca da Rimini* theme under the same description as someone who can see the opening as a vestigial Baroque motive or can give the various chromatic alterations their proper technical names. But she will certainly have her own ways of understanding and describing what happens in the theme, and it is these melodic happenings she is perceiving and enjoying in the perception.

You may reply that I have loaded the dice in favor of my hypothesis by picking so complicated a melodic structure, lasting more than thirty bars and not even closing there, going through numerous and difficult harmonic contortions: plenty of room, of course, for musical thought. But what about the pure melodic impulse of folksong? What about "Green-sleeves"? What can intellect find to chew on there?

Well, one must remember that musical thoughts come at many levels of difficulty and complication; and there is not to think about in "Greensleeves" what there is in Francesca's theme. But clearly no listener will fail, for example, to enjoy the modal quality of the former, although the descriptions of what one is enjoying would vary with the listener's knowledge, from "I like the suggestion of the Dorian mode given by the B♮ (when the melody starts on D)," to "I like that kind of archaic, ecclesiastical quality it has," to Mrs. Munt, perhaps, who likes it because "it sounds sort of old-fashioned."

Perhaps you think I have loaded the dice again: I picked a simple but unusual theme, so of course I have found something in it for people to perceive, think about, and enjoy. How about "Twinkle Twinkle Little Star," a tune with absolutely nothing in it to think about. Well, isn't it becoming quite plain that if one finds a tune that is so simple, so banal, so without interesting or arresting qualities that there is nothing in it to think about, there is going to be nothing in it to enjoy? I am not claiming there are no tunes without something in them to think about; I am not trying to explicate what makes something perceivable as a tune. I am claiming that if someone is enjoying a tune, one is perceiving things happening to the tune, consciously perceiving *that* those things are happening, and how (under some description or other), and enjoying that they are happening in these particular ways. Where those ingredients are absent, enjoyment is absent.

Of course enjoyment comes and goes. A tune may cease to be enjoyable because its perceived elements cease to be interesting and no new ones are discovered to enjoy. Or it may become enjoyable again by new discoveries. I might, for example, rekindle your interest in and enjoyment of "Twinkle Twinkle" by playing you Mozart's Variations for Piano, K. 265, on "Ah, vous dirais-je, Maman" (same tune). For Mozart's conception of the theme and its implications would reveal in it things for you to enjoy that you never knew were there. But show me a tune that offers no object for thought at all—and, by the way, a melody can be interesting just because of its *simplicity*—and you will have shown me a tune that offers no musical satisfaction. This, I think, was the point Glen Gould was making when asked what he thought about some form of rock music of which he apparently had a very low opinion. "What's there to think about?" was his reply.

Objection (4) takes us to the minimal objects of musical appreciation: to timbre and to chord quality in themselves, not as elements in musical works; to the sound of Arthur Grumiaux playing an open string or a three-year-old Mozart whose ear is tickled by thirds. How can these be construed as objects of cognition? What is there to cognize in these simple, formless musical qualities?

It might be useful to recall here a disputed point in Kant's third *Critique* that is well known to commentators on the text. Kant writes, in Section 14, that "a mere colour, such as the green of a plot of grass, or a mere tone (as distinguished from sound or noise), like that of a violin, is described by most people as in itself beautiful, notwithstanding the fact that both seem to depend merely on the matter of representation—in other words, simply on sensation, which only entitles them to be called agreeable."[4] The musical question here, for Kant, turns on whether a tone does or does not possess *form;* for if it does not, and is "mere sensation," then it cannot, on Kant's view, properly be called "beautiful," even though it produces pleasure or satisfaction of some kind. The disputed point, for commentators, is whether Kant thinks the vibrations of air that a tone sets up are perceived by cognition as forms, in which case a single tone could be called "beautiful" on that account; or whether he thinks the vibrations simply stimulate sense, uncognized, in which case they would not be formal properties of tone, as heard, and the tone, therefore, inappropriately called "beautiful."[5] Neither the disputed point in

4. Kant, *Critique of Aesthetic Judgement,* p. 66.
5. It appears possible that Kant changed his mind between the second and third editions of the third *Critique*. On this, see John Neubauer, *The Emancipation of Music from Language: Departure from Mimesis in Eighteenth-Century Aesthetics* (New Haven, Conn., 1986), pp. 188–191.

Kant scholarship nor Kant's theory of the beautiful is directly relevant to my concerns. What is relevant is Kant's apparent denial that musical tones have any perceived and cognized form (apart from the disputed one of vibrations in the air), for it seems to me that, at least in the favored instances, Kant is mistaken. When someone plays a note *musically,* whether on a violin, piano, woodwind instrument, or even a drum, the note is given a "life": it begins, and it ends, and something happens to it in between, both dynamically and with regard to its tone-quality. Thus even in so minimal a musical object as a half-note played with musicality on the G-string, there is formal structure to be consciously perceived and enjoyed: the way the tone swells or diminishes, the way the quality changes from "full-bodied" to "ethereal," the way the vibrato is executed or withheld. There are features to perceive in a well-executed note, and, I believe, they are available for perception, cognition, and satisfaction not merely to the expert but to the ordinary music lover as well. Isaac Stern may hear more in Arthur Grumiaux's tone than I do, and what I hear he may hear under a far more elaborate description. But neither of us merely hears a simple, uniform sound: the accomplished musical performer has learned to make his or her sound "interesting," and the listener responds, quite appropriately, by taking pleasure in its features, perceived under some description or other.

But further, we respond to any stimulus quality as a quality *of* something: the smoothness of a hand-planed board, the iridescence of a cultured pearl, the middle-C of a violin or an oboe. So even if a musical sound were completely simple in experience (which I doubt), it is always the object of musical perception *as* a sound *of* a certain kind, perceived and cognized under some description. And, needless to say, the satisfaction we take in it varies with the description, even if the oscilloscope can't "hear" the difference. The pleasure I take in a sound I believe to be produced by a Steinway grand is different from the pleasure I take in a sound I believe to be produced by a synthesizer's imitation of one.

Chords, of course, are complex objects. When one hears

them, there is always the manner of hearing them not merely as having simple, "emergent" qualities but as having parts one can discern. But even when they are perceived as qualitatively simple—and we are talking here of chords as isolated entities, not parts of musical compositions—they are, like single tones, events with forms as well as qualities *of* something. I will not pretend to know what went on in the three-year-old Mozart's head when he struck thirds at the clavier. Perhaps chords are perceived by infants merely as pleasurable stimuli. When chords, however, have become music to the perceiver, they have become objects of perceptual cognition. Everything I have said previously about single tones is true a fortiori about single chords; and there is no need to repeat it. It will suffice to point out that a triad, executed by three (or more) different instruments or even by one, will provide musical parameters beyond those of one tone produced by one instrument; and the complexity of parameters provides ample field for perceptual cognition.

It would have been easy, let me add, to have conceded single chords and tones to the imagined framer of Objection (4) and admit that here we do, indeed, have sonic stimuli out of which the complex musical objects of cognition are fashioned. I think I could still have the general outline of my account under that assumption. But I am firmly convinced that such a concession would be a failure of nerve. It is important and, I think, liberating to perceive how deeply cognitive the musical experience really is. It is easy to see a retrograde canon as an object of musical cognition. However, the stimulus model of music alone will still haunt us until we come to realize that the simplest musical qualities, those that seemed even to Kant to be pure sensations, are not objects for the nerve endings; they are objects for the musical mind. A musical tone may seem to be some kind of paradigm of the simple, unanalyzably beautiful. I suggest it is nothing of the sort. A musical tone, the smallest particle of musical existence, is beautiful because it is *interesting,* and it is interesting because the musical performer who produces it has imparted a complexity to it that makes it so. If you want to know what a tone without such complication sounds like, electronic technology can produce it for you in all of its pristine purity. It is simple, uninteresting, unbeautiful, unsatisfying, unmusical.

In response to Objection (5), I must, to a certain extent, stand mute on the question of why *Cherchez le thème* is a pleasurable activity. But something can be said in explanation and defense of this position that will, I trust, exculpate me from the charge that in standing mute, I am evading a question in a way that completely compromises my project here.

I take it that a good many kinds of human activity are agreed to be pleasurable, though most of us would be utterly baffled if pressed to explain why. To hit a tennis ball on the "sweet spot" of the racket, follow through, and see the ball whistle over the net is, one might say, inherently enjoyable. Why? What should one say? I do not suggest either that it is somehow inappropriate to ask the question or that there may not be various kinds of psychological, physiological, cultural, even philosophical explanations available. All I wish to suggest is that, for most of us, it would be an adequate explanation of why someone had an enjoyable summer afternoon to say that he or she spent it whistling forehands over the net.

If, on the other hand, the average American observes the game of curling, the activity appears a profound puzzlement. It is particularly difficult to understand what satisfaction can be obtained by the player who runs just ahead of the curling stone, madly sweeping in front of it with what looks like an ordinary household broom. But if the sweeper were to explain to your satisfaction that, when you know the point of the game and have become adept at what he or she is doing, you get the same feeling one gets by hitting a tennis ball on the sweet spot of the racket or catching a line drive, you have, in a perfectly obvious and uncontroversial sense, come to understand the pleasures of curling (at least from the sweeper's point of view).

From the ordinary person's point of view, it is no defect in this explanation that the curler has "merely" made you understand why sweeping is pleasurable by showing you that in certain relevant respects it is like hitting a tennis ball on the sweet spot of the racket. We have been taken from the strange and seemingly unpleasant activity of sweeping—who likes to sweep floors, after all?—to the familiarly pleasant activity of playing tennis, whose charms we know either by direct acquaintance or at least by reliable hearsay.

It is the sweeper's explanatory program that I have adopted here. I hope to show how the activity of appreciating music alone is more or less modeled by *Cherchez le thème* and closely related musical perceptions. I offer no explanation of why such "discovery" is pleasurable; nor, however, do I want to suggest that the question is illegitimate to ask or recalcitrant to reasoned inquiry. But it is a question and an inquiry, as I see it, for others. It is my modest goal, rather, to try to show that the activity of musical appreciation, a cluster of "perceivings that . . ." of which discovery of the theme in the fugue is the paradigm, is agreed on all hands to be the kind of activity that human beings generally find pleasurable. Why they find it pleasurable is an interesting and deep question. On it I stand mute. That silence does not, however, make my explanation of musical enjoyment vacuous or nonexistent. For it is progress at least to have gotten from curling to tennis. And that is what I have settled for here, which will, I trust, acquit me of the charge of standing mute on the question of why *Cherchez le thème* is enjoyed.

I might dismiss the final objection as, after all, asking for too much. Having given what I think is a satisfactory explanation of the pleasure we take in musical features that I can think of, it would surely be a demand emanating from Wonderland to hold me accountable for those which neither I nor my objector can think of, on the grounds they might be there nevertheless. Indeed they might, making Objection (5) truly unanswerable in the final analysis. But I can at least make what I think is a plausible response, short of answering the unanswerable. I will invoke what D. G. C. MacNabb calls, in reference to Hume's philosophical procedure, the "Method of Challenge," which is, as he says, "a method of persuasion, not of proof."[6]

Hume, for example, claims, both in the *Treatise* and in the first *Inquiry,* that all of our ideas are got from sense impressions.[7] He cannot, of course, show how this has occurred in every case, in his lifetime or in a hundred lifetimes. Instead, he simply lays it down as a challenge to the reader to find an idea that controverts his rule.

I have, in the present chapter, tried to show that our enjoyment of music alone is of cognitively perceived musical sound. We take musical pleasure, so I have claimed, in how we perceive musical events to take place. This is a conscious activity, and the music is not an uncognized stimulus to pleasure, like a drug or a tickle, but a cognitive object for us. I have gone through some musical cases. But I cannot, in my lifetime or in a hundred lifetimes, canvass every feature of music I can conjure up or that someone else may in the future. So, like Hume, I will end with the Method of Challenge, and my challenge is simply this: find a musical feature whose enjoyment cannot be accounted for in the way I have suggested. If you do, you will have refuted me.

I have tried here to find my way between the Scylla of seeing music alone as a mindless stimulus to pleasure, which does justice to musical purity at the expense of musical cognition, and the Charybdis of seeing music alone as representational, which does justice to musical cognition at the expense of musical purity. I can offer no further "proof" of my position than a limited number of examples and the Method of

---

6. D. G. C. MacNabb, *David Hume: His Theory of Knowledge and Morality,* 2d ed. (Hamden, Conn., 1966), p. 19.

7. David Hume, *A Treatise of Human Nature,* ed. L. A. Selby-Bigge (Oxford, 1955), pp. 1–7 (Book I, Part i, Section 1); *An Inquiry Concerning Human Understanding,* in Section 2, *David Hume on Human Nature and the Understanding,* ed. Antony Flew (New York, 1962), pp. 33–37.

Challenge can provide. But I can and will offer further explication of it. To that end, I talk next about what some recent philosophers have called the "musical understanding." I shall, in effect, be making the same point I have already made, in a different and, I trust, enlightening way.

CHAPTER 6 /

It's Only Music:
So What's to Understand?

If I were to ask you the question, Do you understand music? what kind of a question would I be asking, and what kind of evidence might I accept for an affirmative answer to it? For it is clear that the question, Do you understand X? would be a very different question, and the evidence for an affirmative answer of a very different kind, depending upon what would be substituted for the placeholder X.

If I asked you, Do you understand German? it is clear what kind of a question I would be asking, and that the evidence directly bearing upon an affirmative answer would be your demonstrated ability to provide paraphrases, in other languages, for German sentences. It is equally clear that scarcely anyone who has thought seriously about music is prepared to take this as a satisfactory model for musical understanding. For it is agreed on all hands that music is not a language in any but an attenuated or metaphorical sense, and that it certainly possesses no semantic content. To provide paraphrases in English of pure instrumental compositions would surely be considered musically unsophisticated in the extreme. Such effusions might, under certain circumstances, be charming literary conceits, but not to be taken seriously as musical analysis.

There is, of course, a related question I might ask about

linguistic "objects," by which I mean literary works of art, that can plausibly be extended to such nonlinguistic art forms as sculpture and painting. I might ask, Do you understand Goethe's *Faust?* or, Do you understand Raphael's *School of Athens?* and expect, as evidence of an affirmative answer, some kind of "interpretation": It is about the value of human striving, or, It is about the reconciliation of philosophy and religion. For we think that literary works can "mean" something, as wholes, beyond what the individual sentences mean that make them up; and at least some paintings, though by no means all, seem to be able to bear such "meanings" too. But, again, there appears to be no foothold in pure instrumental music for that kind of approach. I suppose there is the rare instance. Perhaps it makes some kind of sense to say that Bach's *Art of Fugue* is "about" the fugue, and there are instances in which we might want to say that individual details or large features of a musical composition are "about" music itself. The reader will recognize, in these claims, the notion of music being reflexively "about" itself we met in Kuhns and (more problematically) in Barzun. I do not deny the claims, as broadly conceived, or the presence of such features as Kuhns and Barzun describe, broadly conceived. However, anyone who tried to find such musical interpretations in any kind of thoroughgoing way would quickly come a cropper or enter the airy-fairy land of the Romantic imagination, with music as the revelation of "metaphysical reality," "universal harmony," or whatever else is unintelligible enough to sound slightly mysterious and slightly "musical" at the same time. That way madness lies. We have already met that madness, in our discussion of music alone as representational, and, I hope, exorcized it.

A third kind of question seems more promising. Suppose I were to ask someone, Do you understand clocks? That is short, I take it, for Do you understand how clocks work? And there does seem to be some plausible analogy here to music. For just as a clock contains an intricate mechanism, with all sorts of complex things going on to some overall effect, so a symphony or string quartet, when "taken apart," reveals a wealth of "internal" happenings that one might be tempted to call its "musical machinery." Understanding a string quartet, then, is like understanding a clock: one knows how it works.

[handwritten: don't know musical purpose]

If, however, we press this analogy further, it quickly breaks down. To understand how a clock works, we must understand first what a clock is for: we must know that its purpose is telling time. For we may know that this cog pushes that lever, and that lever pushes the other gear, but until we know how the whole mechanism of cogs, levers, and gears ends up telling the time, we will understand neither the mechanism nor the clock. And here, of course, is where the analogy with music fails, for string quartets, as opposed to clocks, have no purpose at all. If someone were to get up, after listening to the third Rasoumovsky, and ask, What's it for? we could conclude only that he was a man from Mars or someone asking some deep philosophical question, perhaps intelligible but light years away from the question of the purpose of a clock, or a printed circuit, or a can opener.

Well surely, it will be replied, string quartets, and symphonies, and those kinds of things *do* have a purpose: their purpose is enjoyment, appreciation, a pleasurable experience. True enough; and not beside the point, vis-à-vis the musical understanding, as I will suggest in a moment. But first it is important to understand that whatever role enjoyment and so forth play in our account of what understanding music is, we should see that it does not play the role of "purpose" that time telling plays for clocks, short-wave receiving plays for printed circuits, and so on. For *all* of those things can also be enjoyed, appreciated, afford pleasurable experiences. But a string quartet *qua* string quartet, or *qua* music, has no specific purpose at all beyond enjoyment, if that really is a "purpose" in the full-blooded sense of the word (being often thought synonymous with having no purpose at all).

[handwritten: does not play a purpose]

String quartets are meant to be enjoyed, appreciated, experienced pleasurably. As mightily platitudinous and philosophically unfruitful as it might seem, that statement must hold the answer to the question of what we are talking about and asking about when we talk about and ask about understanding music.

How is musical enjoyment related to musical understanding? We have already examined the view, held by many in the past and still, in my experience, widely held today by intelligent and musically sophisticated listeners, that music is a stimulus and musical enjoyment a "natural" response, in much the same way as a drug is a stimulus and the "high" it gives the natural response to its chemical structure. On this view, "understanding music" can only mean understanding the mechanism by which music acts on the human physiology to produce musical enjoyment, as "understanding drugs" means understanding what drugs are made of and how what they are made of produces their particular felt effects. Notice that on this view, I, the listener, need understand *nothing* about music to enjoy it, any more than I need know anything at all about chemistry and human physiology to get drunk. Knowledge is for experts—composers, music theorists, musicologists, critics—and although I may be expert and listener at the same time, my expertise has no more to do with my musical enjoyment than a chemist's has to do with the high he gets when he shoots up on heroin.

I think there is no quicker or more convincing way of refuting the "stimulus-response" view of musical enjoyment than by drawing this conclusion; for surely, whatever view we have of the relation between musical understanding and musical enjoyment, we are no more inclined to think that our enjoyment of music has nothing to do with our understanding it than that our enjoyment of literature has nothing to do with our understanding *it,* however much the two cases might differ in other respects. It seems clear, then, that the question, Do you understand music? cannot be analogous to the question, Do you understand drugs? if you mean by the latter, Do you understand the mechanism by which chemicals have the natural effects they have on human beings? Music just is not that sort of thing, as I have already argued at length.

Let us change our strategy at this point, then, to see if we can finally get the beginnings of an answer to our question. What sorts of things do people who are supposed to understand music really say about it, when they are exhibiting their knowledge and expertise? Leaving the historians of music aside and going to the music theorists, what we find many of them doing, much to the puzzlement of people who take the word "theory" seriously in the phrase "music theory," is giving us very elaborate *descriptions* of music by use of a technical vocabulary that few in the laity understand. And to the extent that "theory" is more than mere description, comprising, among other things, explanation and prediction, for example, music theory of this very common and well-known kind is not "theory" at all. The music theory of which we are speaking is an elaborate and (in some respects, anyway) remarkably precise way of describing musical objects (as compared to the ways we have of describing literary works and paintings). And those who try to talk about music in nontechnical language, the various critics, program annotators, and popularizers, are doing the same thing: *describing* music. To understand music, then, seems in significant part to be able to describe it. And so we accept as evidence for an affirmative answer to the question, Do you understand music? correct and convincing descriptions of it.

But what is the relation of understanding music to enjoying it? I think we want to say that some kind of understanding is a prerequisite for enjoyment. However, that claim seems rather implausible, it might be objected, if understanding music is the ability to describe it. For many people seem to enjoy music who would be hard pressed to offer any description of it. Isn't music, after all, notoriously difficult to describe, particularly for the laity? Yet musical enjoyment is not the exclusive property of the experts. Mrs. Munt enjoys Beethoven's Fifth. Does she understand it? Can she describe it?

Our strategy, as in the previous chapter, will be to go from the complex to the simple, from the expert's description of music to Mrs. Munt's, from technical understanding to common understanding. For here, as with the case of musical thinking and perceiving, it is the simple rather than the complex which is the more perplexing on the account I am trying to give.

I argued in the preceding chapter that the enjoyment of music is an enjoyment *in* perceiving musical happenings under varying descriptions. I am now suggesting that we customarily take a person's musical understanding to be evidenced by, to be constituted, really, by, his or her ability to describe the musical happenings perceived, thought about, enjoyed. This seems to fit in nicely with and, therefore, to confirm the claims made in Chapter 5. I take it as pretty much a matter of common sense that the enjoyment of music is directly related, in a positive way, to the understanding of it, as would be the case with regard to any other of the arts and enjoyed objects of human perception. If that is so, then we can see directly what the relation is between musical understanding and musical pleasure. It is a firm though not infallible generalization that the degree of musical enjoyment increases as the detail and extent of the musical object perceived and (thus) available for appreciation. This is altogether to be expected. The more there is for one to perceive, the more there is for one to enjoy. The degree to which one can describe music, which is the extent and detail of the description under which a piece is perceived, is at the same time the degree to which that music is understood and the extent and detail of the perceptual object being enjoyed: an intentional perceptual object, remember, which the description in effect determines.

I do not claim, it should be cautioned, that there is only one kind of musical theory and analysis, the kind that amounts, in effect, to more or less technical and elaborate description; later on I shall talk about one of the other kinds. But what will, I think, be brought to mind in any musician or former music student by the word "theory" will most likely be the harmonic, contrapuntal, and thematic analysis of tonal music that offers a kind of running description of its vertical and horizontal structure. And when one thinks of evidence for musical understanding, the ability to provide descriptive analysis is, I would suggest, what one ordinarily has in mind. The detail and accuracy of such descriptions give evidence of an intentional object of musical perception that is both more complex and more extensive than the one the ordinary music lover would command. Nor is it counterintuitive to think that the complexity of the intentional object perceived bespeaks a wider, more intense, and more pervasive enjoyment. Clearly there is a relation, recognized by common sense, between enjoyment and knowledge or understanding. If I come to enjoy (say) looking at postage stamps, that enjoyment provides a motive for acquiring knowledge about them; and a direct correlation is hardly surprising, therefore, between enjoying stamps—their contemplation and collection—and knowing about them. But common sense also recognizes a reciprocal effect: the effect of knowledge or understanding on enjoyment. It may be that I am motivated initially to acquire knowledge of stamps because I enjoy their contemplation. However, in knowing more about stamps I can, common sense tells us, enjoy the contemplation of a stamp more than I could theretofore, because I see more in it to appreciate and take satisfaction in. And I see no reason why the case of music should be any different. There is here, as elsewhere, a reciprocal relation between understanding, construed as ability to describe, and enjoyment, increasing with increase in understanding.

But if, as I am arguing, evidence of understanding music is the ability to describe, and enjoying music is a direct function of understanding it, where can Mrs. Munt enter into this equation? Clearly she enjoys music. But it is not at all clear that she understands it, since it is not at all clear that she can describe it.

Well, this seems to be a mirror image of our problem, in the previous chapter, with Mrs. Munt's thinking about music, a precondition we set down for musical enjoyment. And so we already have a strategy for answering it. For Mrs. Munt need no more be able to describe music in music-theoretic terms, to be said to understand it, in her fashion, than she need be able to think about it in those terms, to be said to perceive and enjoy it, in her fashion. All we require is that Mrs. Munt be able to describe the music in the terms under which she perceives it. Thus while Tibby may say "it begins, not with the chord of D, but with that of A, whether major or minor is uncertain, as the 'third' of the chord is left out,"[1] or "the fact is that its opening bare fifth may mean anything within D major, D minor, A major, A minor, E major, E minor, C sharp minor, G major, C major, and F major, until the bass descends to D and settles most (but not all) of the question,"[2] Mrs. Munt will give a "phenomenological" account, in her own words, suggesting the obvious things that ordinary listeners experience in the first bars of Beethoven's Ninth Symphony, such as doubt, anxiety, groping, ambiguity, and eventually the resolution (in the ordinary sense of that word) of those psychological states; but both will be describing the same *sonic* event.

What should be noticed straightaway is that I used the word "sonic" rather than "musical," for Tibby and Mrs. Munt are neither perceiving nor describing the same *musical* event. The musical event is an intentional object, determined in part by our beliefs, descriptions, perceptions of it; and Tibby's musical object, as evidenced by the depth and detail of his description, is a far more complex one than is Mrs. Munt's or Margaret's (which would, I imagine, be somewhere between the two, in that regard).

Novice makes non technical descriptions

A second and important point to notice is that nontheoretical descriptions of music make more abundant use of emotion-, mood-, and psychological state–predicates than any of

1. I appropriate this description from George Grove, *Beethoven and His Nine Symphonies* (New York, 1962), p. 338.
2. Donald Francis Tovey, *Essays in Musical Analysis,* vol. 1: Symphonies (London), 1935), p. 68.

the other kinds. This well-known point is of such great importance to the discussion of music alone that I will devote two
separate chapters to it. For the nonce, we will register the fact
and put it temporarily aside, going on to consider five possible
objections to what I am saying here that, I suspect, will come
initially in mind.

Objection (1). You are arguing that musical enjoyment is a
direct function of musical understanding; and musical understanding cashes out in the ability to describe music. Many
people can, indeed, describe music; but many more cannot,
including, one would think, Mrs. Munt, and Margaret too, no
doubt. But if they cannot describe it at all, they do not understand it at all, on your view. Yet they *do* enjoy it; and musical
enjoyment, you said, is a function of musical understanding.
So your position is contradictory.

Objection (2). Perhaps the two most basic forms of music
"theory" the music student is initiated into are harmonic analysis and species counterpoint. Indeed, both are so integral a
part of training in music, whether one is to become an instru-
mentalist, conductor, composer, teacher, or just a former music student and current listener, that one is very likely to describe the two together as the "grammar" of tonal music. Like
the grammar of a natural language, they comprise the true
prerequisite for understanding.

But the phrase "grammar of music" is not just a felicitous
metaphor. It is not, perhaps, quite literal either; yet it conveys a
basic truth about this kind of music theory and about the music
the theory describes. For music does, indeed, present itself to us
not merely as Kant described it, a "beautiful play of sensations,"[3] but rather as a quasi-syntactical structure: a syntax
without a semantics. In this Kant gave evidence of his palpable
lack of insight into the music of his time, whereas Eduard
Hanslick, seemingly Kant-like in his invoking the "arabesque"

---

3. Immanuel Kant, *Critique of Aesthetic Judgement,* trans. James Creed
Meredith (Oxford, 1911), pp. 188–190.

as his image of pure music, nevertheless recognized, too, the "grammatical" way in which this arabesque of sound is perceived. "By contrast with arabesque," he wrote, "[m]usic has sense and logic—but musical sense and logic. . . . [W]e recognize the rational coherence of a group of tones and call it a sentence, exactly as with every logical proposition we have a sense of where it comes to an end, although what we might mean by 'truth' in the two cases is not at all the same thing."[4]

If, however, music is a syntactical structure of some kind, and the music theory we are talking about its grammatology, then the notion that understanding music is evidenced by one's ability to describe it takes on a familiar and convincing form— but at the cost, apparently, of making Mrs. Munt and her ilk nonunderstanders. For if understanding a language means, in part, being able to describe the grammatical structure of its sentences, then it seems altogether reasonable that, if music has a quasi-grammatical structure, understanding it would mean being able to "parse" it: something that Mrs. Munt cannot do. But if Mrs. Munt cannot give a grammatical accounting of the music she hears, she does not understand about it something that is overwhelmingly important to it; and if she cannot understand that feature, she cannot enjoy it. Whatever else Mrs. Munt may understand and enjoy in Beethoven's Fifth Symphony, if she cannot enjoy its syntactical structure, she is so far from the heart of the matter as to be hardly an enjoyer of the *music* at all. Like Helen, she might just as well be hearing heroes and shipwrecks. And that conclusion is intolerable. It makes music, in one of its most important aspects, understandable and (hence) enjoyable only to the musical grammarians.

Objection (3). The old saying is that ignorance is bliss. And its art-theoretic special case is the frequently expressed fear of analysis killing pleasure. You have suggested that increase in

4. Eduard Hanslick, *On the Musically Beautiful,* trans. Geoffrey Payzant (Indianapolis, Ind., 1986), pp. 29, 30.

knowledge brings increase in enjoyment. Perhaps it does some of the time, but surely not always. Let us grant that increase in understanding is essentially (for reasons already given) the enlargement of the intentional object of perception that is the heard musical work. More features perceived do indeed hold out the promise of more features to enjoy. However, the increase also holds out the threat of features perhaps unpleasant and to be deplored. The search for apples can turn up the rotten as well as the ripe.

You have made it seem as if there is a simple, direct, positive correlation between increase in understanding and increase in enjoyment. That, clearly, is not the case. Increase in understanding may, in the way just suggested, produce *decrease* in enjoyment. The sophisticated listener may come to "see through" those appealing qualities in shallow music which the naive listener enjoys. The sophisticated listener has thus increased understanding but decreased enjoyment. And surely we do not want to deny that someone can understand music while not enjoying it, although we may want to insist that no one can enjoy music without understanding it, at least at some level or other.

Objection (4). And surely, it is bound to be objected, you have placed far too much weight on the verbal description of music as evidence of musical understanding. This emphasis ignores, indeed contradicts, the palpable fact that music is a nonverbal skill, musical understanding a nonverbal, nonlinguistic understanding. In this regard, consider the following obvious cases.

A composer can create the most formidable, abstruse musical structures and yet be completely at a loss to tell us how he or she has done it or even what, exactly, he or she has done. Composers can be notoriously nonverbal and noncommunicative. But it would be bizarre indeed to say that composers do not understand music. Even Wagner, perhaps the most verbal of the great composers, wrote about everything under the sun, Bryan Magee points out, *except* composition, and that because about the composing of music nothing can be said. "Someone unacquainted with his character might suppose this to have been the one area where he felt fully self-assured and therefore not required to explain himself. But of all human characteristics, reticence was the one most alien to him. If he said so little it can be only that there was little he could say. And this can mean only that the music rose to his pen from levels deeper than anything that even he could verbalize."[5]

Pretty much the same thing might be said about performers. There are musicians in whom the ability to perform is so natural, so in-born, such a gift from God or Nature, that it seems more like a natural faculty—like seeing and hearing—than like a learned skill. Granted, no one can achieve mastery of a musical instrument except by dint of application, although some have done so without formal instruction. But to those in whom such potential exists, it comes in a way they cannot describe or account for. Nor, when they perform, can they tell you necessarily what it is they are doing, or how it is they understand the music they are playing or singing or conducting. Performers, of course, vary in their verbal skills and the degree to which they intellectualize their musical interpretations. Surely, though, there are those who can do very little in the way of verbalizing their understanding of music. And, one would think, a magnificent performance of the "Hammerklavier" Sonata is evidence enough that the performer "understands" music, even though he or she might be at a complete loss to describe the music in sophisticated terms.

Finally, anyone who takes lessons on an instrument or attends a master class knows full well that although talking of course takes place, and verbal descriptions of music are offered by teachers, very frequently "words fail," and the teacher finds it easier and far more effective to show rather than tell the nature of a particular passage and how it should be rendered,

5. Bryan Magee, *Aspects of Wagner* (Oxford, 1988), p. 80.

by singing, or playing, or gesturing: in other words, by describing, perhaps, but in a nonverbal way.

In a word, then, music is a nonverbal art, understanding it nonverbal understanding: so the emphasis on verbal descriptions of it seems utterly misplaced or, at least, an overemphasis.

Objection (5). There are many kinds of musical understanding other than the kind you have characterized as the ability to describe music, and many other kinds of music theory to reflect them. Many of them do not seem to fit into your scheme: in particular, some of the many seem to have no direct relation to musical enjoyment, especially that of the ordinary listener; others, though they have a connection with musical enjoyment, in a way, do not connect in the neat way your scheme requires: so even if your scheme is believable as far as it goes, it does not go far enough toward doing real justice to the concept of the musical understanding.

The first objection requires a refinement, for it does point out an uncontested fact. There are many people who enjoy music and who enjoy it seriously; who go to concerts regularly, and listen to phonograph records, and so forth; but who would be hard put to describe a piece of music on demand. What are we to say of them?

Let me begin with what I take to be an analogy from the history of philosophy. When Descartes insisted that all of us have "innate ideas" of things like the equilateral triangle or God, he did not mean, as he replied to his critics, that everyone has these ideas at the ready, so to speak, immediately available to consciousness. They must be nurtured into awareness and may never occur otherwise. I must be "exposed" to mathematics and theology for these ideas to be "exposed" to me. But we may be sure they are there, potentially, to be actualized by the appropriate conditions. (Never mind why—that is nothing to the present purpose.)

In a similar manner, I think we must insist that the ability to describe music may lie in Mrs. Munt in *something* like the manner of a Cartesian innate idea, there to be actualized under the appropriate conditions. But there is a difference. I am certainly not saying that Mrs. Munt's ability, in the sense in which I am describing it, is hard-wired, either by God or by genes. Her ability to describe music is formed in her by her musical experience. As she comes to think about, understand, and enjoy music in the usual ways, she acquires the ability to describe music. So, of course, if she acquires the ability, it is not innate in Descartes' sense. It is "innate" in a relative sense I am about to explicate.

I think I would accept at least two criteria for your knowing how to get to Carnegie Hall: your proven ability to get there—that is, arriving on time for concerts—and your ability to give comprehensible directions. Suppose, now, that you are standing on West 4th Street and 7th Avenue and are asked, "How do I get to Carnegie Hall from here?" Well, you know perfectly well how to do it. You have done it a hundred times. You have a map in your head. You can represent it to yourself. In a sense, you can describe it to yourself. You have an "innate" description of it. You can go through the steps in your mind, one by one: going into the subway entrance, buying your token, getting on the uptown local, getting off at the 59th Street station (even though Carnegie Hall is on 57th), going through that tangle of tunnels so as to end up at 57th St. and not Columbus Circle, turning right at the exit. . . . But now try to describe that to a tourist from Ashtabula, particularly the part about the tunnels. It is hard to give directions: but it's not as if you don't have your facts straight, are inarticulate or illiterate. You have that description right there in the back of your head and can run it over to yourself. It is when you try to make it public, shareable, that things get stuck. You have it on the tip of your tongue, but your tongue just won't cooperate.

Now I want to forestall a possible confusion by contrasting this case with another that is similar. Suppose someone were to ask you to describe walking. Well, you have been doing it every day of most of your life. You surely know how. You surely know what it is like to walk. But can you describe it to someone? I think you would have a problem with doing that. However, your problem here, unlike in the previous case, is that you *don't* have an "innate" description in your head at all, because walking is, of course, second nature to you. You learned so long ago—and then not by having someone describe the process of walking to you but by walking. Walking is an unconscious activity, and we lack a description, either ready or "innate," because of that. I would have to "step back," as it were, to study walking, in order to internalize a description to myself or externalize it to someone else. In the conscious sense, I really don't know what I am doing, or how, when I walk. So how could I possibly be able to describe it?

But this case, I want to insist, is importantly different from the other. I do consciously know how to get to Carnegie Hall. I know perfectly well what I am doing and can represent what I am doing to myself, describe it to myself. What I am having trouble with is not making it plain to myself but making it plain to someone else. Whereas in the case of walking, I cannot even make it plain to myself.

Now Mrs. Munt, I want to argue, is like the person who has trouble telling you how to get to Carnegie Hall, not the person who has trouble giving you a description of walking. Surely she is fully conscious, up to a point, as the giver of directions is fully conscious of how to get to Carnegie Hall, and not as the walker who performs without awareness of what he or she is doing. Indeed, how could it be otherwise? What would the point be of going to hear a concert if one were as oblivious to the music as I am to the phenomenon of my walking, which takes place so many hours of my waking life? When a person does achieve (if that is the right word) such obliviousness to music at a concert, we say that person has lost concentration, has let his or her attention wander; in short, has stopped listening. So whatever Mrs. Munt's problem is, in her inability to describe the music she knows and loves, it is not that she is unaware of what is going on in the music. It is precisely what she perceives as going on in the music that Mrs. Munt is enjoying.

What, then, is Mrs. Munt's problem? And can she, in light of it, be correctly characterized as "able" to describe music, when manifestly she cannot? Her problem, like that of the giver of directions, is that she has difficulty verbalizing her "internal" description. She has the concepts; she has the words; she cannot put them together. In this, clearly, I am not a behaviorist. I do not believe one's having a description means one's being able, here and now, to say it or write it down. The externalizing of it might require prodding of an appropriate kind: "Come on, Mrs. Munt, you know what the music was like: now just relax, think back on it, and describe it in your own words. What was happening in Beethoven's Fifth when you started tapping your foot?" Notice, Mrs. Munt doesn't need a course in music theory, for that would not amount to helping her to the description I am claiming she already, latently, has. Rather, it would be imparting to her a new one, of a more complex and technical kind than the one I am claiming is already in place. What she needs is merely something like the midwifery Socrates throught he was giving to Meno's slave boy to bring forth what was already there.

Perhaps I am treading a fine line here. But I do think it is possible and necessary to distinguish between being able to describe something, in your own words, in the sense of being able right now to do it, and having all of the materials, so to speak, but requiring some preparation or other, some nurturing, in order to give it birth. Would it not be misleading to be behavioristically hard-nosed about it and to claim that Mrs. Munt is "unable" to describe the music she enjoys, just as I am "unable" to describe the internal constitution of stars, on the grounds that neither of us can spew out the right words on demand? I can't spew them out because I know absolutely nothing about astrophysics. She cannot merely because "she isn't so good with words." She *is* able to describe the music,

every child has a Potential to understand music [margin note] only haltingly. Be patient; just give her a little time. She *can* do it.

I do not think, then, that I am ascribing too much to the ordinary listener by claiming that he or she can describe the music in some terms or other. But what about the charge in Objection (2)? Would I be ascribing too much to the ordinary listener in claiming that he or she does indeed perceive, understand, and enjoy the "grammatical" properties of music and can, by consequence of my own theory, describe them? How can that kind of listener describe them? Such a description requires the vocabulary of the musical expert. One needs to be a grammarian to do it. Yet if I deny the ordinary listener the ability to describe these syntactical properties, I deny at the same time the enjoyment of them, since, on my view, perception, understanding, describing, and enjoying are all wrapped up in one package. And to deny enjoyment of the syntactical properties of music is to deny so much as to take away the cat and leave only the grin behind.

Let me begin by pointing out that in music, unlike in ordinary languages, the occurrence of a true grammatical error is rare. Numerous times a day one hears "ain't" for "isn't" and "don't" for "doesn't." But clearly, we do not listen to the music of bunglers and beginners. A syntactical error in any music of the standard repertoire or its peripheries is uncommon and almost always arguable into the bargain. That is to say, we make every effort to be critically charitable and to try to see the "error" as "non-normal" grammar rather than as ungrammatical. In the case of harmonic "lapses," as Janet Levy writes, "[t]he sting or fault of an outwardly awkward or bizarre harmonic progression is removed, or at least, mitigated, by finding a way to understand the problem as a result of (polyphonic) part-writing."[6] We laugh patronizingly at the eighteenth-century harmonists' "corrections" of Purcells' false

6. Janet M. Levy, "Covert and Casual Value in Recent Writings about Music," *Journal of Musicology* 5 (1987), 21.

relations and other "crudities." Of course they mistook a harmonic system or "language," if you wish, different in important respects from their own for an imperfect groping toward, an adumbration of, their own, that, with the wisdom of hindsight, they could clean up for fastidious modern ears. Perhaps the harmonic and contrapuntal crudities of William Billings's hymns and fuguing tunes might come closer to being regarded as syntactical errors. After all, he was, unlike Purcell, untutored and self-taught, in the cultural backwoods. But even here things are not so very clear, since as Billings becomes more and more a part of the canon, albeit a minor figure, his mistakes will come to be seen and enjoyed as peculiarities of style, "original" departures from orthodoxy, and appreciated for their novelty and crude but rugged strength rather than derided as grammatical errors, to be tolerated as unfortunate blemishes on whatever good qualities can be found in Billings in spite of them. It is in the composition student's uncorrected exercises that the real grammatical errors are to be found, and the ordinary listener hardly ventures there.

Now the comparison I am making here, between musical "grammar" and the grammar of natural languages, is not entirely symmetrical. For what I am comparing is the perception of musical "grammar" in musical works of art (and those of a very high order, at that) with the perception of the grammar of ordinary linguistic usage. And I am suggesting that whereas in everyday discourse we have no compunction about identifying various usages as ungrammatical, in musical works we tend to apply a principle of charity, if you will, whereby apparent ungrammaticalities, such as parallel fifths in Billings or false relations in Restoration composers, are, as much as is possible, understood as "grammatical" in a different style system rather than "ungrammatical" in the one in which they might appear that way. I do not deny that this principle of charity might also be applied to the ungrammaticalities of ordinary discourse; I am merely denying that in fact it is, at least in most circumstances.

What, then, are we really talking about when we talk about the perceiving and enjoying of musical grammar? It seems as if we cannot perceive grammar of any kind without the possibility of perceiving the ungrammatical as well as the grammatical. Yet what I have just said seems to rule that out for music. Well, not exactly.

The experience of grammaticality in music is phenomenological: that is to say, we perceive musical syntax as a phenomenal property of the music. Since music does not—except in the most unusual cases—contain true "grammatical" errors, what we perceive is not the correct or the incorrect, for everything is correct. We perceive, rather, the "correct" and the "incorrect" as aesthetic properties of the music. Thus music gives us feelings, impressions of "rightness" or of "wrongness" resolving into "rightness," but what it seldom gives us is a genuine "ain't." If it seems to, it is because we, like the eighteenth-century bowdlerizers of Purcell, have not caught on to the style; have not learned the "language"; have not internalized the "syntax." Let me adduce an example of what I mean.

Here, in Example 3, are some very familiar cadential figures, the first just about as regular a V-I cadence as one can find, the second a simple suspension, the third what is sometimes called (for obvious reasons) a "Corelli Clash," the fourth a diminished seventh.

Now it is perfectly clear that I hear these musical sequences "syntactically," within the musical understanding of that concept. This you can infer directly from my music-theoretic characterizations of them, minimal though the theoretical knowledge displayed may be. The first sequence I perceive (ignoring the suspension over the bar) as an uncomplicated, "well-formed formula," the description "V-I" indicating that I understand its grammatical structure within the style. The description of the second, using the word "suspension," indicates that I recognize a departure from "normal form," a suggestion of ungrammaticality in the dissonance that has, in the end, a syntactically "proper" outcome. One can compare it to

Example 3. Arcangelo Corelli, Trio Sonatas for Two Violins and Continuo, Op. 2

Sonata No. 1

ALLEMANDA. Largo

PRELUDIO. Adagio

Sonata No. 2

ALLEMANDA. Adagio

Sonata No. 3

PRELUDIO. Largo

my knowing that every sentence must have a subject and a verb, and so forth, and hearing the word "Came" as the beginning of an utterance. Something seems slightly askew, grammatically, since the common way to begin a sentence is with the subject not the verb. But when the utterance is finished, "Came I to Camelot," the sense of grammaticality returns with the correct completion of the sentence. For "Came I to Camelot," like "I came to Camelot," fulfills the requirements for a complete, grammatically correct English sentence, although the former is not in "normal form." The dissonance that the suspension introduces, like "Came" at the beginning of the utterance, injects something that gives the initial impression of a grammatical mistake. It is a dissonance, a "wrong note." But it comes right when the dissonance is resolved, as the sentence comes right when its dissonance is resolved by the appearance, at last, of its missing components.

It can now be seen straightaway that the remaining two cadential figures are merely slightly more complicated variations on the same grammatical theme. In each case a seemingly ungrammatical mess is cleared up in the end by supplying the required element, as the seemingly ungrammatical utterance beginning with the impossible "Came" is turned into the complete sentence "Came I to Camelot" by the appearance of the rest of the words.

But so far I have spoken only about my own experience of these simple, musically syntactical features. And I am not the problem, for I possess the requisite concepts. It is Mrs. Munt, and those like her, who seem out of the secret. They do not possess the concepts "V-I," "suspension," "resolution," "diminished seventh," and the like. How, then, are we to say they can perceive the musical grammaticality that is being exhibited here?

The answer lies in our earlier stipulation that the experience of grammaticality in music is phenomenological, that as listeners we perceive musical syntax as a phenomenal property of the music. The perception of "wrongness" and "rightness"

experienced as phenomena

we ascribe to Mrs. Munt is not the perception that a rule has been violated or followed (although that is a perfectly possible way to perceive it). That kind of perception is indeed only to be ascribed to the musical grammarian. But what we can and do attribute to Mrs. Munt is the perception in the music of qualities that seem to her appropriately described in informally syntactical terms. She has a sense of "wrongness" in the altered notes of the diminished seventh, as if someone is "flat" or "off key," and she has the sense of "rightness" when things work out. Of course she has not perceived the "wrongness" and "rightness" under the description "diminished seventh." She has, however, her own words for describing this grammatical property she perceives in the music. This all-important mode of musical perception is what makes music, even to the untutored Mrs. Munt, something other than a kaleidoscope of sounds. For there is nothing of syntax in the kaleidoscope's patterns: nothing is "right" because nothing is "wrong." Were Mrs. Munt unable to participate in musical grammaticality, she would indeed be so musically impoverished as to be scarcely describable as a musical listener. There may be musics without syntax, but Western music is not one of them. And to fail to hear that syntax, at least at some minimal level, would be to almost totally fail to hear the music. Fortunately, however, there is no need to deny that perceptual ability to Mrs. Munt and her ilk. For to hear the grammar of music is, for most but the "experts," to hear just that "phenomenal" rightness and wrongness which any member of our musical culture can hear.

I have, of course, resorted to excruciatingly trivial examples of musical syntax to make my point. And it might be well to observe that the grammatical "wrongness" of these examples may have faded with their familiarity. Like dead metaphors, they may have ceased to give any impression of being out of joint and now give only one of a purely banal "rightness." I trust, however, that that will not be misperceived as a defect in the argument. It is the form of these illustrations, not their content, that makes the argument work. So let them be stand-ins, if necessary, for less wilted flowers, Mahler and Richard Strauss, if you like; although the diminished seventh may still hold some charms for Mrs. Munt.

Now in a sense Objection (3) is well-taken, not so much a refutation of my view but rather an argument requiring something in the way of amplification and qualification. It claims, in effect, that the relation between understanding and enjoyment is not a simple relation; it cannot be stated baldly, as "quantity of enjoyment increases with level of understanding." In this regard the point of the third objection is correct.

How, then, shall we restate, with suitable qualifications, this relation between understanding and enjoyment? We can say, as a first approximation, that *appreciation,* anyway, varies directly with understanding: that is to say, increase in understanding always brings with it increase in appreciation. But appreciation, as I am using the term, is neutral as to pleasure or displeasure. That is to say, by musical appreciation I mean here the propensity of the listener to enjoy or not enjoy, be fascinated with or bored by, like or dislike musical works. And in that sense, musical appreciation does indeed vary directly with musical understanding as I construe it. The more I understand a work, the more I hear in it; and the more I hear in it, the more opportunities do I have for liking or disliking it, being bored by or fascinated with it, enjoying or not enjoying it: the more appreciation, in other words, do I have of it.

But let's look just a little more carefully into exactly how appreciation grows. It grows, I said, through increase of understanding, which enlarges our stock of perceived musical features. Here is a simple but instructive example. Someone who likes and is familiar with Mozart's music may, in his or her sampling of that composer's works, come upon the *Symphonie concertante* in E♭ for woodwinds and orchestra, K. 9A. (There is some dispute about whether this is a genuine work of the master, but the question has nothing to do with the point I am making, so let us assume the composition is *echt.*) The finale is in the form of a theme with variations, the variations being separated by a fairly regular orchestral ritornello, itself varied in its occurrences, to keep them from growing fatiguing. The movement is immediately appealing to anyone acquainted with the style of such music, the musical form and material easily comprehended. A few hearings, however, are bound to reveal that the "variations" of the ritornello consist merely in surface ornament: the musical material is really distressingly alike in each occurrence. This increased understanding of the nuts and bolts of the movement, far from increasing our enjoyment, palpably decreases it. The feature of musical uniformity that is revealed, and added to our intentional object of appreciation, is a disappointingly boring one, a feature to be not adored but abhorred. The ritornello now seems rather tiresome: a rare case of Mozart's invention and craftsmanship failing him (if indeed it is Mozart). Increased understanding has thus brought increased appreciation—but, alas, in the form of displeasure rather than pleasure.

The opposite case, of course, is one in which increase of understanding brings increase in enjoyment. The opening tutti of the Sixth "Brandenburg" Concerto will surely be immediately appealing to the sensitive listener on first hearing. The deep, mellow sounds of the viols, the easy flow of the upper voices, the rich, full accompaniment, all are features that bring instant gratification. What is not so apparent, just because of the consummate ease and lack of perceptible "technique" that characterize the opening, is the fact that the two upper voices are engaged in a strict canon, only one half-beat apart. When this is discovered, there is—or at least there was, in my case— a quantum jump in understanding of, admiration for, and pleasure in the movement. In particular, of course, the technical tour de force of the canon in such close imitation, and (hence) so wonderfully disguised, provides a feature much to be savored (and a feature, by the way, that does not have just "local" significance but casts light on the whole structure of the movement beyond). It is this kind of discovery which exemplifies in the most obvious way the relation between increased understanding and increased enjoyment, by way of the expanding musical object. My intentional object of musical perception "lacked" the canon before discovery and "possesses" it now.

Now these two examples have artificially selected out a negative and a positive feature, respectively. But that, of course, is an oversimplification. At the same time that I am "seeing through" the variation technique in the Mozart ritornello, for example, I may also be discovering pleasing features as well. Any increase in understanding may bring both positive and negative results as far as enjoyment is concerned. And, of course, I cannot back away from musical understanding in order to avoid its possibly negative results, because I could not then avail myself of its positive results either. Understanding (as I understand understanding) is the only game in town. If I don't risk the negative to get the positive, I will never increase my musical enjoyment at all.

Here, then, is what we have to say: musical understanding always increases musical appreciation. But increase in musical appreciation, in any individual cases, may sometimes increase, sometimes decrease musical enjoyment. However, it still might be true that overall, in the long run, increase in musical understanding yields increase in musical pleasure; that in spite of setbacks, the general tendency is for increase in understanding to bring increase in enjoyment. Do we have any reason to think that this is so? I think that we do. The argument is simple. We have good evidence that A enjoys music much more than B does if (i) A listens to music much more than B does; (ii) A talks about music much more than B does; (iii) A expresses his enthusiasms for music (and his animosities against music) much more vigorously and seriously than B does. But isn't that just what is the case with a more knowledgeable listener as opposed to a less knowledgeable one? And the knowledge, let me add, needn't be technical knowledge, merely the knowledge that the music lover has gained informally. The more knowledgeable listener is just the one who has music at the center of his or her life; who listens to it frequently; who talks about it incessantly to anyone within earshot; who "gushes" over music and musical performance long and aloud. This direct and simple correlation between the behavioral criteria by which we judge that someone gets from music intense pleasure beyond that of the ordinary person and the person of knowledge, either technical or informal, beyond that of the ordinary person, strongly suggests the conclusion that in general, if not in every case, increase in understanding of music brings increase in its enjoyment. The curve may not be absolutely smooth, but the general tendency is upward. That is the conclusion in which I will rest, and it suffices for my purposes.

Objection (4) raises some difficult questions, and in the end it will force some qualifications of my view as so far stated. But the qualifications are by no means unwelcome and, in the event, by no means fatal.

To begin with, an important distinction, amounting to a statement of purpose, is in order. This book is about *listening*. It is about the musical understanding of the listener: an aesthetics of musical listening, if you will. It is this understanding—the understanding of the musical listener—that I claim is evinced in the ability to describe music.

There are, to be sure, various other musical activities that require other kinds of musical understanding: composing and performing are the chief among them. Of course, listening is a necessary condition for both, so interpenetrating these activities that one can scarcely prize them apart. Clearly a performer must hear what he or she plays or conducts or sings, in order to evaluate and improve—but also in order to perform at all. When Beethoven ceased to be able to hear adequately, he ceased to be able to perform; and he continued to be able to compose because, with what we must believe was a musical imagination of the highest possible order, he continued to be able to "hear" in his head.

But insofar as composing and performing are activities other than the activity of listening, and certainly they are that, they are quite beyond the purview of my study. They evince modes of musical understanding that may well be quite other than the kind I am outlining here. To put it simply, the composer understands how to compose, and the performer how to perform; and it is scarcely surprising that such understandings do not express themselves in the ability to describe anything.

That composers cannot tell us how they compose, in the sense of how they get their ideas, is, I should add, no more surprising than that scientists cannot, or philosophers, or inventors, or any other "creative" people. This well-known state of affairs is summed up under the now familiar precept that there is no decision procedure for discovery, whether it is artistic, scientific, practical, or any other.

But where it comes to understanding music as a listener, it may well be, although perhaps this has the sound of paradox, that someone other than the composer can evince a deeper understanding of music, even of the music of the composer himself. There should, however, be no paradox here. For I think Socrates' insight in the *Ion* still stands. The creator may draw from he knows not where—the gods, if you like, or the depths of the unconscious, if you prefer—that which those other than he are better able to understand. It is no paradox that Heinrich Schenker—if his theories of tonal music are valid—understood Beethoven's Seventh Symphony better than the composer himself. Of course he did not understand better than Beethoven how to create such a work. And about which is the deeper or more valued understanding there is no dispute whatever. So in saying that Schenker may have understood Beethoven's Seventh Symphony better than Beethoven did we are, of course, not committing ourselves to the claim, that *would* be paradoxical and might be confused with the other one, that Schenker had a deeper understanding of *music* than did Beethoven. (It will, I hope, be obvious to the reader that in speaking of Schenker in this way I am not necessarily endorsing his views, merely using him as a symbolic stand-in for the music analyst at the highest level of achievement.)

Where the composer is a listener, then, his understanding may or may not be of a kind commensurate with his or her compositional understanding. Few composers of the past have left us any extensive evidence on that regard. And we certainly cannot conclude, for example, from the fact that Bach left us virtually no written discussions of music, whereas Berlioz and Schumann left us a great deal, that the latter two were superior in that department. All I suggest is that it is perfectly possible, and no paradox at all, that Bach (whom I consider the greatest musical intellect of modern times), although an order of magnitude or more deeper than Schumann in musical understanding *sans phrase,* may have been—although I have absolutely no reason to believe he was—inferior in what I have been characterizing as listener's understanding. In any case, we know that Schumann was outstanding in this regard, through the music criticism he left us and that we continue to read with pleasure and profit.

Let me conclude this discussion of the composer's musical understanding by emphasizing that nothing it has so far revealed tends in any way to cast doubt on my account of the listener's musical understanding. For where it exhibits features other than those I have indicated as belonging to the listener's understanding, such features appear to be not of the listener's understanding at all but of the understanding of the composer *qua* creator. And of that I have nothing to say. But where we consider the composer *qua* listener, there seems nothing that does not conform to the notion that the musical understanding evinces itself in the ability to describe.

What of the performer? I can get at that question best by going to the final point made in Objection (4), concerning the nonverbal description of music.

Let me begin by saying straight out that I by no means deny there are nonverbal ways of describing music. Let me also add a cautionary codicil to that. A gesture or a sung or played phrase may at times be worth a thousand words of description—but only when it has been preceded by a good many words. Musical thought is *thought,* musical understanding *understanding.* And whether or not one believes that thinking is linguistic through and through, one can hardly stray very far from language without feeling that one has perhaps strayed from thought as well.

The listener's understanding, then, is evinced through the ability to describe the intentional object of his or her musical enjoyment. That description can certainly be nonverbal as well as verbal. Even the person who can play no musical instrument whatever can sing and gesture in ways that supplement verbal description. A description in gesture, song, or instrumental performance, no less than a description in words, tells us "the way things go." So one can, perhaps at times to better effect, say "the place where the theme goes dum-dum-diddle" rather than "the place where the theme descends in seconds and thirds."

Now if I can partially describe the "Hammerklavier" Sonata (say) by humming a segment of its melody, which is after all the act of minimally performing a minuscule part of the composition, it would seem to follow that a complete performance of the work, on the instrument for which it was originally written, would be a complete description of it. But that is absurd, you may say. A performance of the "Hammerklavier" isn't a description of the thing, it's an instance of it; or (to de-Platonize the objection) it's the thing itself. Let me try to convince you that it is not absurd to think of a performance as a description; that it is, rather, illuminating and consistent with what I have been saying about musical description and musical understanding.

To start with, we can immediately blunt the seeming absurdity by observing that there is absolutely no reason in logic for not believing that the "performance" can be two things at once: both a description of the "Hammerklavier" and an instance of it or (if you prefer) just *it.* And that indeed is what I want to suggest. One can and, of course, usually does understand and appreciate the playing of a piano sonata as a performance of it. But one can also, if one wishes, understand the playing as a description. How, and to what end?

Another word to describe a musical performance is "interpretation." It suggests that a performance of a work must be motivated by and encapsulate a particular understanding of the work. What that understanding is, in words, is of course a description of the intentional object of the musical perception of the performer *qua* listener. Some performers may be better able than others to articulate their interpretations verbally as well as musically. Some may be almost completely unable to verbalize their interpretations, able to "describe" them only by their playing or singing or conducting. But if a firm interpretation is embedded in the playing or singing or conducting of a work, then a listener with a sensitive ear and linguistic skills can hear it, "read it out," and, further, articulate it, even if the performer, being nonverbal, cannot. In that act the listener is essentially using the performance as a "description" of the "the way the music goes." It is part of what we call music "reviewing"—or should be, anyway, when that much maligned enterprise is brought off well.

Thus it is no paradox to think of a performance as the ultimate nonverbal description of the work. That is not *all* it is; but it is, among other things, that. Some of the performer's understanding, of course, has nothing to do with having an idea of "how the music goes"—having, that is to say, an "interpretation." A great deal of it is "knowing how": knowing how to play an even scale, to play polyphonically, to use vibrato, to play in tune, to get a good sound, and so on. Such knowing, of course, is musical understanding as well, as is the composer's knowing how to write a fugue, or harmonize a chorale, or orchestrate a symphony. But it is not the understanding about which I write. I write of the listener's understanding; and that understanding, in the performer, is evinced most fully, most characteristically, in the nonverbal description that we call his or her interpretation—which is to say performance—of the musical work.

This leaves me with Objection (5), and a formidable objection it is. For there is no gainsaying the many ways of "understanding" music and the many things called "music theory." To even begin to cover them all would require a separate book many times the length of the present one. And it is very doubtful that every kind of musical understanding would fit into my scheme, anyway, or every kind of music theory. Prudence would suggest backing off completely from this issue. But, it seems to me, I have taken so many risks in this book already that one more won't matter much one way or the other. So at the risk of having the worst of two worlds, I am going to devote, not another book, but the next chapter to discussing briefly another kind of music theory with a view to saying how it does, and does not, and *should not* fit into my scheme.

CHAPTER 7 /

Surface and Depth

In the previous chapter we looked at the kind of music theory most familiar to those who have gotten, in their musical training, the standard course in basic musicianship. It is, as we have seen, hardly anything like the things that the word "theory" usually brings to mind but, rather, turns out to be an elaborate kind of description, in a technical language, and can best be characterized as a kind of syntax or grammatology.

What *does* the word "theory" tend to conjure up? And is there anything in music like that?

Well, of course, to most of us "theory" means "science"—so it is scientific theories that we think of as the kinds of things theories are. But scientific theories or explanations (if that comes to the same thing) themselves come in many shapes and forms. Few philosophers of science would, I think, endorse the view that there is only one kind of explanation or theory properly called "scientific." But there certainly is one kind of scientific theory or explanation that will be very familiar to all; in form it was already known to the Greek atomists. It is the kind of explanation that attempts to account for some perceivable, gross property of something on the basis of its inner structure: for example, Lucretius's explanation of the viscosity and liquidity of fluids in terms of the roughness or smoothness of the "atoms" he imagined material substances to be composed of. This kind of explanation or theory does seem to have some analogues in some of the things music theorists do, usually under the head of "analysis." How exact this analogue might be, and what significance such musical theories might have for the normal listener (and for the view being propounded in this book), are the subjects of this chapter.

But to begin such a discussion we first have to get a clearer idea of just what the kinds of theories or explanations I am talking about are like. Of course these are deep waters. However, I see no need to plumb the murky depths. So I will rely on an account aimed at a lay audience in John Searle's splendid little book *Minds, Brains and Science*, his Reith Lectures for the BBC.

In the first of these lectures, Searle wants to distinguish between two ways in which a cause can be related to its effect. Crudely, "It is tempting to think that whenever A causes B there must be two discrete events, one identified as the cause, the other identified as the effect; that all causation functions in the same way as billiard balls hitting each other." But a far more sophisticated model of another kind of causal explanation is one in which cause and effect are not distinguished in this way: a kind of explanation in which the inner structure of some material substance or system is said to be the cause of its own properties. "I think the clearest way of stating this point," Searle writes, "is to say that the surface feature is both *caused by* the behaviour of micro-elements, and at the same time is *realized in* the system that is made up of the micro-elements. There is a cause and effect relationship, but at the same time the surface features are just higher level features of the very system whose behaviour at the micro-level causes those features." Thus, for example, "the solidity of the table in front of me is explained by the lattice structure occupied by the molecules of which the table is composed."[1]

---

1. John Searle, *Minds, Brains and Science* (Cambridge, Mass., 1984), pp. 20, 21.

Physical science is devoted, as Searle points out, to the distinction between the macro- and microstructure of matter: the former is constituted by those properties we have dealings with in our everyday lives ("the solidity of the table in front of me"), the latter by those properties or entities which scientific theories postulate as explanations of the former ("the lattice structure occupied by the molecules of which the table is composed"). Now music too, although it is a crafted rather than a natural object, might seem to exhibit an analogous distinction between surface and depth structure. For there is, first of all, the musical surface that we hear and enjoy in our listening, whether we are casual listeners like Mrs. Munt, serious ones like Margaret, or even educated ones like Tibby. But might there not be also a "microstructure" beneath that phenomenal surface, analogous to the molecular structure of the table and perhaps like it in some way explanatory of what we hear at the surface? Can we "look" closer at the music to locate this inner core? There are musical analysts or theorists (if you like) who seem, in what they do, to assume something very like the scientist's distinction between macro- and microstructure, surface properties and deep properties, and a causal connection between them. I will examine one such analyst, and the musical reader may or may not want to extrapolate what I have to say to other similar writers with whom he or she may be familiar.

What probably springs at once to the mind of the educated musical scholar will be the work of Heinrich Schenker and the school of Schenkerian analysis it gave rise to. For it is a signal feature of Schenker, and of his numerous active followers, that they purport to see beneath the surface of tonal music in the West a generative element, the *Ursatz*, which vibrates (if you will pardon the image) with overtones of scientific explanation.

I cannot deal with the Schenkerian model here. It has the aura of cult about it and has developed a musical language and discourse all of its own that must be mastered before it can be evaluated fully. Such an undertaking would take us too far afield. All I can say about it here is that if the reader finds anything hereafter relevant to his or her understanding of what Schenker and his followers were and are about, well and good; if not, I am also content.

What I would like to discuss is a kind of thematic analysis practiced most notably by Rudolph Reti but by no means unknown before him or abandoned since. And I introduce it with a completely uncontroversial—indeed trivial—example.

As is well known, Haydn grew fond, in later life, of what is sometimes called monothematic sonata form. For example, we often find, in the first movement of a late Haydn symphony or string quartet, that the themes—first theme, second theme, closing theme—are not completely different tunes, as in many sonata movements, but each a different version of the same tune or, if you will, the succeeding themes "variations" of the opening one. Example 4 will illustrate the point. I quote what I take to be the complete first theme (measures 1–16) and complete second theme (measures 49–64) of the first movement of Haydn's last symphony.

The first thing to notice may at this point seem trivial in the extreme but will later prove of no little importance. The two themes, although very nearly alike, except for key transpositions, of course, are not literally the same, having different endings. It is doubtful that this near identity would need to be pointed out to a listener of Margaret's sophistication, let alone Tibby's, although perhaps Mrs. Munt might need to be prodded. In any event, if, like Humpty Dumpty, someone needs to see it worked out, we show him or her that the first theme and the second theme of this movement are the same theme by chopping off their endings. Through this (trivial) operation we arrive at two melodic tokens of the same melodic type: in other words, the same tune.

I take it that the following things are pretty obvious and uncontroversial: that the second theme of this movement is a slight variant of the first theme; that Haydn consciously

Example 4. Joseph Haydn, Symphony No. 104 in D Major, First Movement, Exposition

planned it that way and intended these tunes to be heard as versions of each other; that this relationship between the two themes is a "real" aesthetic property of the work; and finally, that coming to perceive these themes as the same gives to the movement a coherence it would not be perceived as having prior to one's perceiving the thematic unity of these tunes. To tell someone that the first movement of this symphony is, in the sense explained above, "monothematic" is to give that person what I take to be a paradigmatic musical "interpretation," or at least part of one (where, that is, we are dealing with pure music, with music alone).

But now an obvious question will arise. If the thematic unity of the Haydn first movement is supposed to give it coherence, what of a movement without such monothematic structure, of which there would seem to be so many? Haydn liked monothematic sonata form. Mozart did not resort to it as often. Yet Mozart's movements in sonata form (at least the better ones) are also perceived as coherent. Thus the general question arises, to quote a recent musical analyst: "How do we explain the musical as well as the psychological feeling of unity sensed in the great works of Mozart, Haydn, Brahms, Beethoven?"[2] Not all of these works seem to possess what is called monothematic structure, exemplified by the first and second themes of the first movement of Haydn's Symphony No. 104. Yet all of them seem to possess coherence. How is that to be accounted for?

Just as the Haydn movement raises the question, so it suggests an answer. If a structure, palpably monothematic, gives the Haydn movement its sense of coherence, might not monothematic structure, hidden, buried, unknown, and unperceived, give coherence to musical works not palpably monothematic but perceived to be coherent? Not only does the Haydn movement suggest this answer, it suggests the method for verifying it. For even where the structural relation is excruciatingly obvious, as in the case of the first and second themes of the Haydn first movement, we have been introduced to the way it may be demonstrated to the skeptical: which is to say, the operation of transformation by which, in either adding notes to themes or subtracting notes from them, we reveal the themes' true identity, making them two melodic tokens of the same melodic type. Nor need we confine the

2. David Epstein, *Beyond Orpheus: Studies in Musical Structure* (Cambridge, Mass., 1979), p. 3.

procedure to demonstrating the monothematic structure of individual movements. For the same method of transformation can be applied to themes from a whole work, as, for example, in Rudolph Reti's analysis of Beethoven's Ninth Symphony (of which more in a moment), or even to themes of a group of works, as in Deryck Cooke's article, whose title is self-explanatory: "The Unity of Beethoven's Late Quartets."[3]

The lengths to which this "method" of transformation can be and has been taken is best brought home with an example. Here is how Reti tries to demonstrate the thematic relations between the first theme of the first movement of Beethoven's Ninth and the celebrated "Ode to Joy" theme of the last movement. He begins by dividing the first movement theme into ten segments (arabic numerals 1–10), which are all transformations of four more basic segments (roman numerals I–IV). Letter "a" marks the staff on which the original theme is notated; letter "b" the staff on which are notated "its four motivic elements," after the removal of inessential notes. It is to these "elements," already the result of the method of transformation, that the "Ode to Joy" theme will be related in the succeeding analysis, after further transformative operations (see Example 5).[4]

Compare, now, in Example 6 the first subject of the first movement of the Ninth with the well-known theme of the finale. (The measure numbers are Reti's).[5]

It is hard to imagine two more unrelated and vividly contrasting themes, in either structure or mood, as the angular, jagged, leaping first subject of the first movement and the fluid, vocal, hymnlike theme of the ode. Reti recognizes this and does not fail to comment upon it. "The theme has changed to a tune," he

3. Rudolph Reti, *The Thematic Process in Music* (London, 1961), pp. 11–30; Deryck Cooke, "The Unity of Beethoven's Late Quartets," *Music Review* 24 (1963).

4. Reti, *Thematic Process in Music*, p. 11.

5. Ibid., p. 16.

Example 5.

says, and indeed, "the transformation has gone so far that on the surface it is no longer discernible as such." But such "surface" dissimilarity hardly daunts Reti, for "the *underlying* triad suffices to assure us of the basic homogeneity.

How, then, do we reveal the identity of two such seemingly nonidentical themes? By removing the inessential notes that

Example 6.

disguise it, beginning with the notes that obscure the triad, for "the original triad . . . is filled with bridging notes, thus making it fluent, songlike." Other of the motifs that, as Reti sees it, make up the first subject of the first movement are revealed by further transformational operations: "The ascending and descending thirds of motif II appear as interwoven subphrases in the melodic course. In fact, they form, transposed and at original pitch, the very bridging notes by which the triad is filled to produce the tune of the 'Ode.' Motif III is indicated by lifting the theme from D, E, F-sharp, G (bars 10 and 11). Motif IV, finally, the descending seventh, is expressed through bars 11 and 12."[6] Reti supports this claim with an illustration, quite revealing of his method, which I quote as Example 7.

As this juncture I want to beg a question and make a point. I suggested, in discussing the first movement of Haydn's Symphony No. 104, the following model. A listener, if he or she is naive enough, a Mrs. Munt perhaps, might hear the movement and miss the fact that the first and second subjects are the same tune except for the final three measures. Were I to point out that feature to the listener, he or she would then, in future hearings, perceive that relation between the first and second themes as part of his or her listening experience of the music. And thereafter the music would seem to the listener more coherent, more unified than before.

What Reti and others of his kind are doing, I want to urge, *seems* to be in sharp contrast. And the model it most readily suggests, on first reflection, is the model of scientific explanation with which we began this chapter: the accounting for perceivable macroproperties by recourse to an imperceptible microstructure. For what such analysts begin with is the datum of perceived coherence. As Donald Mitchell says, in a prefatory note to Reti's *Thematic Process in Music*, "We talk about unity and undoubtedly experience it every time we lis-

6. Ibid.

Example 7.

ten to a masterpiece, small or large." This is the macroproperty that demands an explanation. Reti, Mitchell believes, has given us (almost, it seems to be suggested, like a Newton unraveling all) "the 'how' of it." And how he has given the "how" is to explain it in terms of a monothematic structure beneath which, on Mitchell's view, *the composer did not intend us to hear.*7 I emphasize this point because it makes explicit what is clearly assumed throughout Reti's analysis, that we do not perceive this understructure as part of our aesthetic experience of the work even *after* the musical "atomist" has revealed its presence. Rather, it is the unexperienced cause of the coherence or unity that we do perceive, as the lattice-structure (unperceived) of the table, in Searle's example, is the cause of the table's (perceived) solidity.

Is this the correct way of representing what Reti and his kind are up to (regardless of what they think they are up to)? Do we have here a "science" of music? If we do, it is very bad science indeed, as a moment's reflection on its "method" will reveal.

Let us critically reconsider the process by which Reti tries to convince us that the "Ode to Joy" theme of the Ninth is a "transformation," a version of the first movement's first subject. In particular, I want to look at how he gets the scale structure of the former from the triad structure of the latter, and how he gets measures 11 and 12 from motif IV, the descending seventh.

To make a scale into a triad, what you do, of course, is remove the intervening notes. But what rationale do we have for determining which to remove and which to leave? A com-

7. Ibid., pp. v, vi.

mon and obviously reasonable procedure is to remove the "inessential passing tones," that is to say, the ornamental notes that do not belong to the chord they are coming from or the chord they are going toward; for since the chords accompanying the melody may be assumed to mark the essential points of melodic structure, the removal of the inessential passing tones can reasonably be seen as a procedure for revealing the basic (harmonic) structure of the tune.

The trouble for Reti is that this quite sensible and commonly accepted procedure will not get the results he wants, will not "reveal" the triad in the scale. That is to say, just removing inessential passing tones will not transform the ode theme into triads. Reti claims that "[t]he kernel of its opening," which I assume to refer to the first two-and-one-half measures, "is the triad in D." To get the "kernel"—that is, the triad in D—Reti must remove the G in measure 1, the G in measure 2, and the E in measure two, thus giving the D-major triad (see Example 8).

But a look at the first harmonized statement of the theme—in which, one has a right to assume, its harmonic structure will be spelled out—reveals deep problems for Reti's analysis. The G in measure 1 goes without a whimper, for it can be seen as a dissonant appaggiatura resolving to the fifth of a D-major chord. However, in measure 2 it is the A that is the nonchordal tone, a dissonant appaggiatura resolving to the root of a IV chord in the first inversion; and both the F# and E are chordal tones, the third of a tonic chord and the root of a II chord, respectively (see Example 9).

Even if we give Reti the removal of the E for the sake of the argument, he still does not have his triad. For what the harmonic analysis reveals, even giving Reti the benefit of the

Example 8.

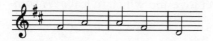

Example 9. Ludwig van Beethoven, Symphony No. 9 in D Minor, Op. 125, Finale

doubt, is that the basic structure of the first three measures is not the triad but, rather, Example 10.

Thus the rationally justifiable criterion of removing non-chordal tones will not do Reti's job. What rational criterion will? The answer seems to be "none." The only criterion that will do the job—the one indeed which we must assume to have been employed, implicitly, to be sure—is simply that of removing or adding any note whatever until you get what you have already decided is there.

The same "method" can be seen at work in getting measures 11 and 12 of the ode theme from motif IV of the first movement's first chapter (see Example 11).

The problem here is to show that there is "in" the ode theme a descending scale from the sixth degree to the seventh below it. To show it, Reti inserts his scalpel at what seems a most unlikely place, one-and-one-half beats into measure 11, in the middle of a ligature. Now the G is a chordal tone, the third of a II chord; so harmonically it has some legitimate claim to being a "core" note of the theme, whereas the F# does not, being, obviously, a nonchordal passing tone. How-

Example 10.

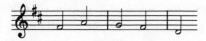

Example 11.

ever, the E has, from the harmonic point of view, an equally legitimate claim. And if one takes the melodic as well as the harmonic parameters into consideration, it seems at least arguable that the F# and G are an ornamental flourish, the E the important structural note, which would be made all the more obvious if one considered how the melody should be phrased in performance: surely with an accent on the E, at the beginning of the measure, not on the G, on the second half of the second beat. Furthermore, even if we give Reti this extremely contrived starting point, in my view not musically justified at all, he can get only four of the notes he wants. The fifth note, an ascent of a whole tone, must be chopped away, the fifth, sixth, and seventh notes added, in order to get, literally, a major version of motif IV. Or, eschewing pedantic literalism, one must be satisfied with having gotten to the area of the dominant as a near-enough approximation. Reti rests content with the conclusion that "Motif IV . . . is *expressed* through bars 11 and 12," "express" a term broad and vague enough, in this context, to cover a multitude of sins. Now if I am permitted to pick any point in a melody I wish, leave out or add any notes I wish, of course I can get motif IV from measures 11 and 12. I can, indeed, get anything from anything: to appropriate a nightmare of Nelson Goodman's, "Three Blind Mice" from Beethoven's Fifth. This is not science; this is astrology. It is the well-known fallacy of finding what you want to find by putting on your "finding" technique no restraints at all except the restraint of never allowing it to fail to "find" what is wanted.

Schenkerians are particularly anxious to defend themselves against the charge that their own procedures for revealing the *Ursatz* are methodologically shabby ones, being keenly aware of the danger. As one recent defender of the faith puts it, "a Schenkerian approach encourages the discovery of rela- tionships (possibly unexpected) by 'reading through' diminu- tion to underlying shape, but with the restriction that the 'reading' process must be informed by principles that are inde- pendent of any specific configuration one may believe 'ought' to be present."[8] I do not know and will not inquire whether Schenkerian analysis succeeds in fortifying itself against the fallacy of finding what you want to find, as the writer just quoted believes. But I have no doubt at all that Reti and his kind find what they want to find in just the disreputable way warned against above, that of reading the score by principles that are not independent of the specific configurations they antecedently believe ought to be present. No reputable science could proceed in such a way. Eugene Narmour, an outspoken critic of Schenker and his followers, sees in Schenkerism what he calls a biological metaphor harking back to nineteenth- century teleology. I have seen in Reti and his kind a different but also scientific metaphor. And reading "scientific" (in the sense of this chapter) for "biological" (in Narmour's sense of the word), I can do no better, in passing my final judgment on Reti's analysis as a "science," than to quote Narmour's judg- ment on Schenker's as "biology": "But enough of the biolog- ical model: Nature's work and man's, after all, are not directly comparable."[9]

As science, then, Reti's analysis seems utterly worthless. But is it science at all? It may indeed bear some superficial

8. John Rothgeb, "Thematic Content: A Schenkerian View," in *Aspects of Schenkerian Theory*, ed. David Beach (New Haven, Conn., 1983), p. 41.

9. Eugene Narmour, *Beyond Schenkerism: The Need for Alternatives in Music Analysis* (Chicago, 1977), p. 40.

resemblance to the kind of scientific theory that explains macroproperties in terms of microstructure. On the other hand, this may be a misleading analogy. So perhaps we would do better to entertain a more familiar possibility. Nature's work and man's, after all, are not directly comparable, as Narmour says. And one obvious difference is this: nature's work we explain, man's work we can also *interpret*. Here, surely, it is musical interpretation we are dealing with.

Going from scientific explanation to artistic interpretation has, I suppose, some immediate comfort, for we do not demand the kind of rigor from the latter that we do from the former—that is something of a truism, if not a cliché. But such comfort is short-lived. We do, after all, demand reasoned argument of some kind from interpretation, and that demand of course is part and parcel of our belief that interpretations, no less than scientific claims, are to be evaluated. And whatever we may mean when we say that science is more "rigorous" than criticism, we do not, I think mean to say that we will accept logical fallacies, non sequiturs, circular reasoning from the latter any more than from the former. So even if Reti's analysis may look immediately more respectable as interpretation than as science, we cannot avoid the issue of whether it really is respectable or not.

In specific terms, let us put the question this way. Is what Reti claims to be in the music in it after all? That is to say, does his "method," his "argument," carry conviction?

There is, to begin with, a very quick and trivial answer. If you perform the operations on the "Ode to Joy" theme that Reti does, you will indeed get what Reti gets. That is an incontestable fact. The triad is "in" the "Ode to Joy" theme in something like, I suppose, the way in which the statue is "in" the unworked block of marble: remove some stone and the figure is "revealed." Remove some notes with an eye to revealing the triad, and the triad will be laid bare. Is this enough, though? What weight are we putting on the "in" in asking whether the triad *really* is "in" the theme?

One very tempting reply would be the familiar (and contentious) appeal to the composer's intentions. Surely, it might be argued, if Beethoven meant the triad of the first movement's first subject to be heard in the ode theme, then indeed it is there. If not, not, Reti's "operations" to the contrary notwithstanding.

It should be noticed, straightaway, that if we can determine on independent grounds Beethoven's intention to have the triad heard in the "Ode to Joy," this does *not* of itself settle the matter; for the further question arises as to whether we actually hear it there. Once we have moved from "science" to "interpretation," the claim is not that the unheard triad buried in the theme somehow causes the sense of coherence we get. It is that once having come to hear that triad in the ode, we find that hearing it becomes a contributory factor in our sense of coherence: which is to say, hearing that the triad of the first movement's first subject is "in" the ode theme is, to that extent, hearing that there is a coherence, a unity between them. Hearing the triad in both instances *is* hearing coherence or unity. But clearly, the intention that we hear the triad in the ode theme is not self-fulfilling: an intention may fail of its object. And I believe that if Beethoven intended to have us hear the triad or motif IV in the "Ode to Joy," he failed. We see them when we perform Reti's operations on the notes. We do not hear them thereafter in future listenings to the work— that, at least, is my experience. Intentions, then, may be a necessary condition for Reti-like thematic relations being in a work. They are not, however, sufficient.

But to press the point further, could such thematic relationships have been intended? I think they could not. It is not hard to see why. We conclude intention, most usually, by something like an argument from design. If I find on the beach an object visually indistinguishable from a marble bust of Julius Caesar, my most plausible conclusion is that the object is the result of human intentional acts, not of the winds and the tides. On the other hand, if I find an object visually indistinguishable from a pebble, it is more likely that it is the result of natural processes; not because it is impossible for it to have been produced by human intention, as it is impossible in the strongest sense short of logical impossibility to imagine a marble bust of Caesar so produced, but rather, to appropriate Laplace's famous phrase, because we have no need of that hypothesis.

We can now readily see why it would be unreasonable (although not logically contradictory) to conclude that the thematic relationships Reti perceives in the Ninth Symphony are the result of intentional acts on Beethoven's part. It is simply that we have no need of that hypothesis. These relationships are the inevitable result simply of composing in the tonal tradition in which Beethoven plies his trade. It is not a surprise they are there, but it would be if they weren't. It is their absence that would require intentional explanation, not their presence, which is to be expected as the result of "natural causes." This is not, of course, to say they are "natural phenomena." They are, indeed, the results of intended compositional acts, but they are not intended results; and applying the doctrine of "double effect," a Catholic casuist, we may be sure, would declare the composer innocent of their production. (The number of occurrences of the letter "e" on this page is the result of my intentional acts, but it was not my intention to produce that number of them.)

It might be useful to compare the thematic relation that Reti sees between the ode theme and the first movement's first subject with that (which all would see) between the first and second subjects of the first movement of Haydn's Symphony No. 104. Surely there can be no doubt that Haydn intended the second subject to be a version of the first; for the chances of two themes being so alike unintentionally arc as low as the chances of the winds and the tides producing a look-alike bust of Julius Caesar, whereas the kinds of thematic "relationships" that Reti discovers in Beethoven (and elsewhere) would result whether directly intended or not; no intentional hypothesis is therefore required or, indeed, reasonably entertained.

We have, then, in such analyses as Reti and his kind produce, a sort of interpretation that plays havoc with the ordinary notion of interpreting a text as revelatory of what its
author or maker intended it to mean or be. What sort of
interpretation is this?

The rejection of intention as a critical criterion is, of course,
nothing new. William Wimsatt and Monroe Beardsley and the
"intentional fallacy" come immediately to mind.[10] But there
are more affinities, perhaps, in the arcane, beneath-the-surface
quality of Reti-like analysis—something completely absent
from the New Criticism—to what Arthur Danto has described recently as "deep interpretation." In what we might
think of as ordinary interpretation, "understanding what an
author as agent and authority at once could have meant is
central," and "*for just this reason*, must be distinguished from
the sort of interpretation, hermeneutic or what I shall desig-
nate *deep* interpretation, which I want to examine here. It is
deep precisely because there is not that reference to authority
which is a conceptual feature of what we may as well call
surface interpretation." It is in such hermeneutic, riddle-solv-
ing deep interpretation that "it may be justifiably said that the
interpreter knows things the author does not" (psychoanalytic
interpretation being the most obvious case in point).[11] It is
similarly true, I would urge, of the assertions Reti makes
about thematic relationships in Beethoven's Ninth, and elsewhere, that "the interpreter knows things the author does
not." For that Beethoven ever entertained beliefs about such
relationships, ever "knew" or "believed," in that sense, that
they were there, seems to me extremely doubtful. Yet they are
"there," if you will accept their being "there" on the basis of
Reti's somewhat shady operations.

What, then, are we finally to say about these interpretations
of musical works? Is the critical chutzpah of presuming to

10. See William K. Wimsatt, Jr., and Monroe Beardsley, "The Intentional
Fallacy," in Wimsatt, *The Verbal Icon* (Lexington, Ky., 1954).

11. Arthur C. Danto, "Deep Interpretation," in Danto, *The Philosophical
Disenfranchisement of Art* (New York, 1986), pp. 50–51, 52.

educate Beethoven about the musical content of his own works adequate rationale for rejecting such deep interpretations? Not obviously: I have argued in the previous chapter that there is no "paradox" in thinking the analyst *qua* listener may understand the work more deeply than the composer *qua* listener. In literary circles, where textual meaning is the issue, opinion is divided about the relevance to interpretation of authorial intent. And one wonders whether, where interpretation of music alone is the issue, the complete absence of questions about meaning might favor one side or the other and help force a resolution. That is a point worth pursuing, but I shall not do so here. Rather, I want to suggest a further consideration that should, whether or not the relevance of intention is decided, provide some grounds beyond intention for evaluating the kind of deep interpretations of musical works we have been talking about.

It has been argued by anti-intentionalists in literary criticism that one can intend a text to mean something and fail: fail, that is, to fashion a text that succeeds in embodying the intended meaning. Others have argued that no matter how inept, ungracious, or even unintelligible a text may be, it cannot fail to mean what the meaner intended. But we have seen that the intention to give music structural coherence—if by that one means, as I do, structural coherence that can be heard and, further, be heard as part of a musical experience—is by no means self-fulfilling, as some believe the intention to mean might be. If, indeed, Beethoven intended to be heard, and experienced as part of the musical fabric of his work those things which Reti, by something between alchemy and incantation, managed to conjure up there, it must be put down as one of his infrequent musical failures (nor would his failures be infrequent if Reti worked his way with the rest of Beethoven's music, as there is no doubt he thought he could). For what Reti "reveals" has absolutely no effect on our listening: it is "there," to be sure, but no more heard as part of our musical experience, after the revelation, than a statue is seen in an unworked block of marble, for all the assurances of the sculptor that it lies beneath.

Intention is not enough. What is intended to be heard and musically experienced may or may not be susceptible of being heard or musically experienced. What this fact about intention may well suggest, given the difficulty of independently determining intention anyway, is that the test of any deep musical interpretation will be, in the last analysis, a pragmatic one. If it bakes no bread, it claims no authority. What, when revealed to us by the musical theorist, cannot be integrated into our listening experience of a work is, for all intents and purposes, not a part of the work: not something available for musical perception, musical appreciation, musical enjoyment. For those who may believe that presence or absence of compositional intent is irrelevant to the evaluation of a musical analysis, this pragmatic standard will remain the ultimate court of appeal. And those for whom intention does make a difference will, I dare say, find listening success, plain and simple, better evidence of present intention than anything so airy and philosophical as the version of the argument from design that I offered above.

A rider to this conclusion must, however, be attached. Composers have, in certain periods, intentionally put devices into their music with no intention at all of their being heard—devices indeed that it is quite impossible to hear. The music of the late Middle Ages abounds in them. The reason for their presence is perhaps, as James Anderson Winn puts it, that "[i]f men and Popes could not hear the higher music of such relations, God could."[12] But whatever the reason, it must be pointed out for present purposes that we, in light of such practices, cannot conclude merely from the fact that something cannot be heard that its presence in a score was not intended by the composer. We cannot even conclude that it was not intended to be heard, since we want to allow for the possibility of failed intentions in that regard. What can, per-

12. James Anderson Winn, *Unsuspected Eloquence: A History of the Relations between Poetry and Music* (New Haven, Conn., 1981), p. 105.

haps, be concluded, at least provisionally, is that, in the absence of any external or internal evidence to the contrary, if something cannot be heard, it was not intended to be heard. And as the present essay concerns the musical work as heard, what cannot be heard is not a part of the work, nor is what was not intended to be heard.

This stipulation has the implication that many musical devices of the fourteenth century, for example, are not parts of the musical work as I understand it here. But I hope this notion will not raise too many eyebrows. For I do not mean to say the last word about what the musical work is. I merely stipulate what it is for the purposes of my argument, which is an argument about what we musically hear and what we understand and enjoy in the hearing.

Another kind of music "theory," then, comes down in the end to description, successful or unsuccessful as the case may be. For all of their scientific appearance, Reti's analyses, and those of others like him, are interpretations of art works *qua* artifacts not explanations of them *qua* natural phenomena (although I am not arguing the latter is impossible in principle). If I am mistaken about those I have discussed, if they are in fact successful interpretations, then they have opened up to us heretofore unperceived and unappreciated features of the works they treat of for us to contemplate, understand, enjoy. If I am right, they are failed attempts to do that very thing. In either case, they fall within the ambit of the thesis I am putting forth in these pages.

Two caveats in conclusion. I have not argued that a "scientific" understanding of music is impossible or misguided. Nor do I want to be understood as claiming here, any more than at the conclusion of the previous chapter, that what I have discussed constitutes all of the things that might be properly called "music theory"—not even that I have discussed the most important or the most paradigmatic examples. What I have discussed I have discussed—that is all.

Much more might be said on both of these topics. But it is

time to move on to other pressing matters too long deferred. For it must come as something of a surprise and a felt gap in my argument, both to the musically literate reader and to the laity, that so far I have said nothing positive, or even negative, about the role of emotion in the pure musical experience. Time out of mind, after all, the emotions have played such a prominent role in musical speculation that one would have a right to expect discussion of them to make an early appearance in a work such as this. So to the vexed question of the emotions in music we must now turn, for a long and somewhat belated look.

CHAPTER 8

How Music Moves

*summary of essence of corded shell
music moves in emotion parallel to life ?*

An "ancient quarrel" runs through the philosophy of music. It concerns the relation of music to the emotive life, and I will characterize it here as the quarrel between musical "cognitivists" and musical "emotivists" (if I may be allowed to appropriate terms from another "ancient quarrel" in the history of philosophy).

Those I am calling musical emotivists believe that when, under normal circumstances, musical critics, theorists, or just plain listeners call a piece of music (say) "sad," it is because it makes us sad when we listen to it; and what they mean by "sad" music, I will assume, is music that normally arouses sadness in the normal listener. The musical cognitivists, like the emotivists, believe that it is proper sometimes to describe music in emotive terms. But unlike the emotivists, they do not think that sad music is sad in virtue of arousing that emotion in listeners. Rather, they think the sadness is an expressive property of the music which the listener recognizes in it, much as I might recognize sadness as a quality of a dog's countenance or even of an abstract configuration of lines.

Unfortunately, the quarrel between musical emotivists and musical cognitivists all too often seems to involve a sort of moral crusade. On the side of those who think sad music makes us sad, it is the crusade against heartless, emotionless, analytic listening to what ought rather to be a sublime emotional stimulus. On the side of those who think sadness is a property of some kind that we recognize, that we hear, in the music but do not feel, it is the crusade against wallowing in seas of emotional treacle while the truly musical passes by unnoticed. I take the cognitivist point of view here, as I do on other points throughout this book, but I reject utterly the notion that I am committed to a coldly analytic response to music. I do not claim that the second movement of the *Eroica* does not *move* us emotionally, only that it does not move us to *sadness*, its predominant emotion. Musical cognition and musical emotion are not, in other words, incompatible.

Ever since musical cognitivism came on the philosophical scene as a viable alternative to the arousal theory—which, it appears to me, was sometime in the eighteenth century—it has been resisted, in spite of its (to me) palpable philosophical advantages, because, in part, it was seen by many to present a passionless picture of the musical experience quite at odds with common sensibility. But it is a mistake to think that because sad music does not sadden us, there is no difference between sad music that does and sad music that does not move us and engage our emotional responses. It is the difference, of course, between the great and the trivial, but not the difference between what saddens us and what does not; the great and the trivial both fail to do that.

How far back we can trace the claim that for music to be moving it must arouse the emotions we identify in it, I do not know. But is already at the center of the argument in the efforts of the Florentine Camerata, and its "theoretical consultants," to establish a monodic vocal style. For it was just the signal virtue of accompanied solo singing, they claimed, as against the complex polyphony of the sixteenth century, that the former was moving and the latter was not; which is to say, solo song could arouse, so they thought, the individual emotion of the text it expressed—hope, love, fear, anger, and the like—while polyphonic music in four, five, or more parts could not.

Once the mischief was done, of conflating our emotive descriptions of music with our descriptions of music as "moving" or "not moving" (as the case might be), the "ancient quarrel" was in place. For if one wants to maintain that emotive descriptions of music apply at all, the alternatives then become either to deny that music arouses such emotions as rage, hope, love, joy, sadness, and the like, at the cost of denying that music can be moving (the "coldly analytic" posture); or else to assert that music can arouse these emotions, and does so when it is moving, at the cost of explaining *how* music can do such a thing and *why* we should want to listen to it if it does. (Why should I *want* to be sad or angry?)

The question of *how* has been scrutinized so many times that it may seem pointless to do so yet again. But I am afraid I must, at least briefly; for there is a lesson to be learned from it that, I believe, has not been learned yet and is essential to my argument.

It was apparent to the Camerata in the sixteenth century, and to everyone else since then, that *if* music arouses such emotions as anger and fear, love and hate, hope and despair, sadness and joy, *as a normal aesthetic function*, some special explanation is required to tell us how the thing is accomplished. We all have a general idea of how such "real life" emotions get aroused in us, in our everyday intercourse with our fellow human beings. But music does not seem able to supply the necessary "emotive materials" that these experiences do. When Uncle Charlie, for the one-hundredth time, tells the story of how Aunt Bella was the cause of his failure in business, which I know to be a self-serving falsehood, I feel my anger rise, and I resist the impulse to punch him in the nose or give him the dressing down he deserves. I "know" *why* Uncle Charlie makes me angry, and *how*; and I "know" who I am angry *at*: Uncle Charlie, of course. All of these essential conditions however, seem to be lacking in the situations in which I would describe a piece of music as "angry" and as "moving"—situations in which, the emotivist insists, the music is moving me to anger. Who or what am I angry *at*? At the music? At the composer? *How* was I made angry by a structure of artfully put-together sounds? And *why*? Where's the Uncle Charlie?

There is no Uncle Charlie, and the emotivist knows it as well as I. So at this point he winds up and tries to throw a theory past me: a theory of the emotions, often at what he takes to be the cutting edge of research in the "behavioral sciences." In the sixteenth century it was the theory of "sympathy," in the seventeenth century the Cartesian *esprits animaux*, in the eighteenth century the association of ideas, in the nineteenth century God knows what, and in the twentieth, conflict theories, psychoanalytic theories, behaviorist theories, physiological theories, and, distressingly, sympathy theories once again.

I am not going to discuss any of these theories, which range from the wildly false through the uselessly true to the highly controversial, except to remark that "scientific" theories of the emotions come, and they go; and there seems to me to be something deeply wrong with the way they are put in the service of musical aesthetics by the emotivists. I have nothing against the scientific study of the human psyche or against scientific theories of emotion per se, and I am certainly not arguing that because we do not yet have a successful psychology and physiology of the emotions (if that is indeed true), we can never have one. I think I would be a rash intruding fool if I were to pass judgment, a priori, on the possibility of a behavioral science, and I have no intention of doing so. Rather, what I want to bring out is the peculiar—not to say questionable—position such theories have always been in vis-à-vis the problem of musical arousal.

In a perfectly obvious way, I have a satisfactory explanation of why and how Uncle Charlie makes me angry. Does that mean that a "scientific" theory of the emotions has nothing to add? I hardly think so. Depending upon what kind of a theory it is, it can broaden, deepen, and, perhaps, even replace my Uncle Charlie explanation. But the point is, there is an Uncle Charlie explanation already in place before psychology comes along to deepen it, broaden it, and (perhaps) replace it. I don't need science to tell me that Uncle Charlie gets me angry by telling those fibs about Aunt Bella or that a good way to keep from getting angry is to stay out of his way as much as possible. In other words, although I may not know everything there is to know about the dynamics of my emotional relationship with Uncle Charlie, I don't stand dumbfounded before it as if it were a divine mystery. Uncle Charlie gets my goat, and I know why.

The point to be noted here, however, is that for *music* we don't have the Uncle Charlie explanation at all. We are in need of "psychology" right from the start. That is what bothers me. We are told by the emotivist that music moves us by making us sad and angry, hopeful and happy; yet it seems so remote from the things that usually do that for us—the Uncle Charlies and Aunt Bellas—that it requires some sort of esoteric explanation to make it believable.

Sometimes, of course, our emotions are very real and very mystifying. We can all understand my anger at Uncle Charlie. But if someone customarily flew into a rage at the mere mention of Niagara Falls, as in the old vaudeville routine that Abbott and Costello worked to such perfection, we would have good reason to be puzzled and might, indeed, seek the help of "scientific" psychology to explain *why* and *how*. And there might well be musical cases like that. If, by some chance, I knew someone who became enraged every time she heard Brahms's Second Symphony, I might very well think myself in the presence of a pathological condition that required psychoanalytic untangling.

But why should *all* musical cases require esoteric psychology for their arousal power to be made believable? *That* is *unbelievable*. Music, after all, is a perfectly ordinary part of our culture's furniture and of the furniture of every other culture we know anything about. Surely it is as ubiquitous as our Uncle Charlies and Aunt Bellas. No less ordinary and widespread is our tendency to describe music as "sad," "happy," "yearning," "angry," *and* "moving." If, as the emotivist claims, music is moving in virtue of arousing such emotions as sadness, joy, anger, yearning, and the like, it seems absolutely extraordinary to me that there should be no obvious, commonsensical explanation, of the Uncle Charlie kind, to explain how the arousal takes place. If I had no other reason to be suspicious of the claim that to be moving, music must make me sad, and angry, and yearning, than that there is no ordinary, nontechnical explanation for why these emotions are aroused in me, or how, I would consider the absence of such an explanation enough to put me off that claim. That there are others, thoroughly familiar off-putting reasons as well, such as that no sensible person would want to feel many of the emotions music is said to express, and that there are no behavioral symptoms of listeners actually experiencing them when attending to music, is for me decisive. Placing these other, familiar reasons aside for present purposes, I will indeed make it the central requirement, here, of an account of how music moves that it include an Uncle Charlie explanation: that, in other words, there be a perfectly ordinary explanation, of the kind we use every day to explain why we are angry at this or depressed about that, for why we are moved by music in any particular instance. If music arouses an emotion or emotions in me, it must be, I claim, in the commonplace way Uncle Charlie rouses my ire. Scientific or esoteric explanations may come later to deepen, broaden, or perhaps even replace my explanation of how music moves, as they may do also for the rest of my emotive life, according to some philosophical psychologists. But unless the ordinary psychology is in place first, musical emotion sounds to me more like pathology than like art.

At this point we need to guard against two closely related

misunderstandings. First, I do not mean to suggest that everything under the sun requires an Uncle Charlie explanation.
That is to say, I am not some kind of skeptical defender of
"common sense" against all scientific, philosophical, or other
"esoteric" explanations. Second, I am not, I do not think,
guilty of an inconsistency in having offered an esoteric, which
is to say philosophical, explanation of how music is expressive
of the garden-variety emotions in my earlier book on the
subject.

As to the first point, an Uncle Charlie explanation is required for the claim that music arouses the ordinary emotions
just because emotive arousal is a common, everyday affair and
the ordinary conditions under which ordinary human beings
have emotions aroused in them are familiar to us all, well
understood on the commonsense level, part of our "informal
psychology." (How could they not be?) Thus if music, a common everyday part of our common everyday lives, aroused
garden-variety emotions such as anger, fear, love, and the like
in us, it would seem wondrous strange that it wouldn't do so
in the ordinary, Uncle Charlie way. Where an emotion is
unexpectedly aroused in bizarre circumstances by highly unusual objects or events, esoteric explanations are I dare say in
order. But where the circumstances and objects or events are
as familiar as the concert hall, record player, and music of
one's own culture, part of one's surroundings since babyhood,
the lack of an explanation in ordinary, "folk-psychological"
terms for the purported arousal of the garden-variety emotions seems convincing if not, perhaps, absolutely conclusive
evidence that no such arousal takes place.

On the other hand, to revert to the second possible misunderstanding, although people do seem to find certain nonsen-
tient objects expressive of the garden-variety emotions, "tinged" with emotive color and including, I and others believe,
music, this is not a commonplace fact, nor do we seem to have
any agreed-upon explanation of how these things are or have
become expressive. It therefore becomes a "philosophical" or

"scientific," in other words "theoretical," question how they are and have become expressive of the garden-variety emotions. I have tried to give such an explanation in *The Corded Shell*. But because there is no Uncle Charlie explanation for the phenomenon, so far as I know—and how could I *not* know, if it were truly an Uncle Charlie explanation?—I see no reason why one should be expected or required to provide one for the expressiveness, in this sense, of music any more than for an account of what causes cancer. Thus it seems to me that, in arguing as I have, I am guilty neither of being a scientific and philosophical Luddite, who scorns all artificial contrivances, nor inconsistent in resorting to such contrivances where necessary.

If we are to circumvent the false dichotomy that the emotivist and cognitivist have traditionally pressed—between music as arousing emotions like anger and fear, and being moving on that account, or as presenting those emotions as properties of the music to be heard but not felt, and hence forfeiting the claim to be moving—we must separate entirely the claim that music can arouse emotion in us from the claim that music is sometimes sad or angry or fearful: in other words, we must keep apart the claim that music is *expressive* (of anger, fear, and the like) and the claim that music is *arousing* in the sense of *moving*. As I shall argue later, a piece of music might move us (in part) because it is expressive of sadness, but it does not move us by making us sad.

Two authors have at least partially succeeded in separating questions of what I call *expressiveness* in music from questions of what I call music's power to be *moving*. They are wide apart in time and in outlook but are, I believe, two of the most sensible people ever to have written about musical subjects. Johann Mattheson's magnum opus was *Der vollkommene Capellmeister* (1739): a compendium of practical and theoretical knowledge for the education of the Lutheran church musician. In it Mattheson carefully distinguished, I believe, between the composer's task of *representing* the individual emotions of love, anger, hope, despair, and so forth, in his music, and his task of *arousing* in his listeners love of virtue and hatred of vice, which was his true calling as a composer in the service of the church.[1] For, as Mattheson put it, "it is in the true nature of music that it is above all a teacher of propriety."[2] Thus if I am correct in my interpretation of Mattheson on these points, he can be described as claiming that music moves not in virtue of arousing such emotions as love, anger, and the rest but in virtue of moving the listener to moral approbation and blame. And so he has kept clearly separate the expressiveness of music, which he places in the representation of the garden-variety emotions, from what I would call its power to move the listener emotionally, which he locates in its religious function as, essentially, a musical sermon. He is, so far as I know, the first to make such a clear distinction between music's power to be expressive and its power to move the listener. Unfortunately, his example was not followed, and his position was consistently misunderstood.

Mattheson's distinction is a step in the right direction, but it clearly will not do, for his position on how music moves cannot be right. It may perhaps be the case that some music—(say) Bach's church cantatas—can succeed in teaching a moral lesson, with, of course, considerable help from the texts. But even in these cases I doubt seriously that when we say this music is moving we mean that it moves us to love virtue and disapprove of vice. And surely we *can't* mean that when we are talking about music alone. All would agree, I am sure, that the first movement of Mozart's Quintet in G Minor, K. 516, is deeply moving; but it teaches no moral lessons at all—how could it?—and arouses nothing that could possibly be construed as a "moral emotion."

More promising is the sharp dichotomy that Leonard Meyer

1. For a detailed account of Mattheson's views in this regard, see my "Mattheson as Philosopher of Art," *Musical Quarterly* 70 (1984).

2. Johann Mattheson *Der vollkommene Capellmeister*, trans. Ernest C. Harriss (Ann Arbor, Mich., 1981), p. 104 (I, iii, 54).

maintains, in the opening chapter of *Emotion and Meaning in Music*, between emotions depicted in music and emotion aroused by it. He writes:

> A clear distinction must be maintained between the emotions felt by the composer, listener, or critic—the emotional response itself—and the emotional states denoted by different aspects of the musical stimulus. The depiction of musical moods in conjunction with conventional melodic or harmonic formulas, perhaps specified by the presence of a text, can become signs which designate human emotional states. . . . And it may well be that when a listener reports that he felt this or that emotion, he is describing the emotion which he believes the passage is supposed to indicate, not anything he himself has experienced.[3]

Again, I think the distinction is vital; and the general drift with regard to musical expressiveness, which is to say, music presenting the individual emotions of love, anger, despair, and the like, rather than arousing them, is congenial to the cognitivist's way of thinking about these things.[4] But when it comes to an account of how music arouses (as opposed to denotes) emotion, Meyer commits what I have represented here as the cardinal sin: he relies on a technical "theory" of the emotions, an updated version of John Dewey's so-called conflict theory, to do the business. It is the theory whose "central thesis" is that "emotion or affect is aroused when a tendency to respond is arrested or inhibited."[5]

As I have remarked, theories of the emotions come and go, and certainly if the conflict theory is supposed to be either a "scientific" theory of the emotions or a "philosophical" analysis of them, it is nowhere near the cutting edge of research. Whatever it is, it seems open to the most obvious counterexamples. I don't think anyone will have difficulty thinking of

3. Leonard Meyer, *Emotion and Meaning in Music* (Chicago, 1956), p. 8.
4. My views on this regard are spelled out in Kivy, *The Corded Shell: Reflections on Musical Expression* (Princeton, N.J., 1980).
5. Meyer, *Emotion and Meaning in Music*, p. 14.

cases in which affect is aroused by "a tendency to respond" being "arrested or inhibited" (I am angered or frustrated by the rebuff of my amorous advances); but, contrariwise, I don't think anyone will have difficulty thinking of cases in which affect is raised in the complete absence of an arrested or inhibited tendency to respond (I am overjoyed and elated by my advances finding no resistance at all). Counterexamples of course invite responses that "explain them away," either by asking you to look more closely at whatever it is to see how it "really" exemplifies what theory requires it to, or by asking you to construe the terms of the theory in some way other than the way you are used to construing them. Often you are asked to do both at once, and just as often, when you are finished, the theory has become vacuous; for, as Antony Flew so unforgettably put it some years ago, "A fine brash hypothesis may thus be killed by inches, the death of a thousand qualifications."[6] But whether the conflict theory of the emotions yields to qualifications or to counterexamples, it will be just as dead in either case.

Put aside, though, the question whether or not the conflict theory is a true theory of how emotions are aroused in our everyday lives. Perhaps it is just a true theory of how emotions are aroused by music, of how, as I put it, music moves. Even so understood, however, it will not wash. Meyer's book is full of ingenious examples to illustrate how he believes music arouses emotion or affect by generating and then blocking tendencies to respond. But even if these examples are convincing, there is no end of music that, at least for my money, is deeply moving yet lacking in the kinds of things Meyer takes to be examples of frustrated or blocked responses to musical stimuli. Frustration is no more the sole cause of emotion in music (if it is a cause at all) than it is the sole cause of emotion in our ordinary lives.

---

6. Antony Flew, "Theology and Falsification," reprinted in his *God, Freedom, and Immortality* (Buffalo, N.Y., 1984), p. 73.

But anyway none of this is to the present point, which is that whatever turns out to be the true "scientific" theory (or one of the true theories) of human emotion, music presents it (or them) with a peculiar anomaly. For when the true psychology finally comes along, it will be able to tell me the awful truth about what *really* is going on when I think I am being made angry by Uncle Charlie's prevarications, and the story it tells may be so different from mine that the old one will fall by the wayside as possession by demons did with the advent of the germ theory of disease. But music will present the triumphant psychology with nothing to explain more deeply or more broadly, or to explain away, about how it arouses fear and anger, despair and hope, joy and sorrow, and the rest; for we have no Uncle Charlie explanation in place for how such emotions could possibly be aroused by "organized sound." We are at a complete loss. That is why the emotivist grabs desperately at every new "theory of the emotions" that comes down the pike, in the vain hope of finally finding one that will grind out the desired result.

We will discover how music moves only when, first, we disassociate that question from the question of how music can be expressive of the garden-variety emotions, as Mattheson and Meyer have done; and second, as an inevitable result of that, stop resorting to science (or, worse, pseudoscience) to explain a perfectly ordinary phenomenon of the emotive life that must have a perfectly ordinary explanation, of the kind we resort to every day when confronted with the Uncle Charlies and Aunt Bellas of our world. The explanation is right in front of our noses, there for all to discover.

Let me return for a moment to the place where, I believe, the conflation of musical expressiveness with musical arousal first became obvious. When the early composers of opera and their theoretical spokesmen claimed that Renaissance polyphony was not moving, but that their own music was, they were saying something that on its face seems palpably absurd. For, to take but one example, surely the music of Josquin des

Prez is some of the most stirring music ever to have been composed. What is true of a lot of it, and what was being no doubt confused with the lack of power to move, was that it is not *expressive* music: that is, most of the time it does not present, as part of its musical fabric, such expressive qualities as anger, fear, despair, hope, and the like. Rather, a good deal of it has a kind of sublime serenity that defies description in such emotive terms. Nor is this an accident, for the composers of this music were following an entirely different "aesthetic" (if you will) of text-setting. The new aesthetic of the Camerata had as its goal the *representation* in music of passionate human utterance. But the Netherlands polyphonists' goal was different: namely, placing religious words, which they treated as precious gems, in equally precious musical "settings." If the early baroque composers were painters of passions, Josquin was a jeweler of texts.[7]

I am listening now to Josquin's incomparable setting of "Ave Maria"; and let us say, for the sake of the argument, that I am listening to it played on instruments rather than sung, so as not to muddy the waters by the obtrusion of a text that, no doubt, does have the power to arouse specific emotions such as love or reverence, particularly in the religious listener. This music is as deeply moving as any I have ever heard. How can I best describe what is going on between me and it? I think that if I can describe what is going on here, where there is no danger of my confusing what is expressive with what is stirring (since, by hypothesis, nothing is expressive), I will have a model that can be applied to other cases as well.

Now if I am "stirred" or "moved" by this music, I presume it is fair to say that I am experiencing an emotion. And con-

7. A qualification is necessary here. Some of Josquin's musical compositions were much admired in his time for, and held up as models of, vocal expression in music. In that he pointed forward to the new aesthetic of the late Renaissance, he was, perhaps, transitional. But his work as a whole and the composition of which I am writing, the "Ave Maria," conform, I believe, to the characterization I have given.

emotion reflection of life

temporary wisdom in such matters has it that normally, if this is so, my emotion must have an object: that is to say, my emotion must be toward or about something or other. And I must have some belief or set of beliefs about that something which makes it plausible for me to be described as having that emotion I am experiencing.[8] So, to return once again to my much maligned Uncle Charlie, the object of my anger is Uncle Charlie, or Uncle Charlie's supposed lying, the belief that explains my anger my belief that Uncle Charlie is indeed lying—and, as a matter of fact, lying with evil intent. (There must be other relevant beliefs as well, but I am oversimplifying here.) What, then, is the object of the emotion that Josquin's "Ave Maria" stirs in me, and what the attendant belief or beliefs?

Well, clearly, the object must be *the music*—or, when we refine things a bit, various features of the music. And the attendant beliefs must, it would seem, then, be beliefs about the music. What beliefs would those be?

Imagine that I am a music lover but relatively unsophisticated about the Netherlandish style: someone like I imagine Margaret to be. What will probably appeal to me in my first encounter with the "Ave Maria" is the sheer beauty of the sound as it unfolds in its ebb and flow. I will be moved by sheer beauty of sound, and the belief on which my emotion is predicated will simply be the rather uncomplicated conviction that what I am hearing is very, very beautiful.

But if my sophistication increases, I will, no doubt, next become aware of the perfection of the part-writing; I will perceive with what incredible freedom Josquin can combine melodic lines so that each seems beautiful in itself and yet all fit together in one euphonious whole. My excitement increases with this discovery. I am now moved not merely by the sheer beauty of the sound but by the incomparable beauty and

8. The locus classicus for this kind of analysis is Anthony Kenny's *Action, Emotion and Will* (London, 1963). For a more recent exposition of the view, see William Lyons, *Emotion* (Cambridge, 1980).

craftsmanship of Josquin's counterpoint as well. The object of my emotional excitement has become more complex: not sheer beauty of sound alone but consummate polyphony, with all that implies (although I needn't, as I have argued previously, master the technical language of music theory to achieve such appreciation). And my single belief that these sounds are very, very beautiful has now begun to expand into a system of beliefs about the features of that sound: the freedom of the part-writing, the wonderful voice-leading, the masterful preparation of cadences, the building up of musical climaxes. Certainly enough to wonder at, *and to be emotionally excited about* (which is my point).

But there is more to come. I may, one way or another, come to discover eventually that part of this seemingly effortless, freely moving combination of melodic lines has been achieved under one of the most severe artistic constraints a composer can impose upon himself: strict canonic writing (in the "Ave vera virginitas" section). Not only that. The kind of canon Josquin chooses is of the greatest difficulty: a canon at the fifth with the voices only one beat apart. (It is because the imitation is so close that the canon is so beautifully disguised, the contrapuntal tour de force that it represents so seemingly effortless.) Once discovered, the perception of this canon cannot fail to escalate still further the emotional excitement the listener experiences toward the composition. Again, we find further objects of our emotion and a further multiplying of attendant beliefs. As perception, understanding, the extent of the musical object, and enjoyment of it increase, in the manner described at length in these pages, so too does emotion.

This, then, is my Uncle Charlie explanation of how Josquin's "Ave Maria" stirs me emotionally; how it elicits the emotional response I describe as "being moved by" music. It fulfills all of the requirements I laid down for such an explanation. It is of the common, ordinary, everyday variety that I customarily use to account for my anger at this, my depression about that, my excitement over the other. It makes no appeal to any technical, "scientific," or other esoteric theory of the emotions. It tells me what the object or objects of my musical emotion is or are; and it spells out the background beliefs that make this emotion plausible—the very kinds of beliefs I have been talking about throughout this book. Further, it can be generalized to cover any musical example, just so long as we remember that music of different periods, in different forms, genres, and styles, will provide us with different objects and (necessarily) different background beliefs about them.

There is no need to run through more cases. It will be readily apparent, I think, how the same exercise can be performed with the most diverse musical examples. We will be moved by different things in each. But in every case we will, to give the most general description possible, be moved by the beauty or perfection of the music.

But although, as I say, there is no need to spell out in detail how each such case might be handled, I cannot resist pointing out just one relevantly revealing kind of instance. That is the kind of instance in which some *expressive* property is involved. Let us imagine that we are listening to a piece of mournful music that moves us deeply. The emotivist says that the music moves us by making us mournful. I say this is not the case; rather, the music moves us by various aspects of its musical beauty or perfection. But surely, the emotivist is bound to retort, it is utterly perverse for someone to claim that the mournfulness of deeply moving music has nothing whatever to do with our being moved. And so it is: most perverse. However, it is a perversity that the cognitivist is not in the least committed to. On the contrary, the cognitivist, although he does not think that the mournfulness has *everything* to do with why a piece of mournful music is moving (if it is), thinks that it usually has a great deal to do with it. What, among other things, I am moved and excited by in the last movement of Brahms's First Symphony is the beautiful way in which the composer embodies the expressive properties of mournfulness, anxiety, and expectation in his musical fabric (in the introduction) and then how, at just the right moment, manages the emergence of that gloriously joyous yet resigned and tranquil theme in C major. (I shall spell out more fully the role of expressive properties in the musical experience in the following chapter).

Notice, too, that there is another side to this coin. A great deal of music possesses all sorts of expressive properties but is not moving at all. Georg Philipp Telemann, for example, wrote yards and yards of mournful music, but it would be bizarre to describe very much of it as "moving." Yet on the emotivist's account, that is just what we would have to say, for on that account the music is mournful in virtue of arousing mournfulness in listeners, and moving for the same reason: it is, for the emotivist, a contradiction in terms to impute any expressive property to a piece of music and deny that it moves. Whereas the cognitivist is committed to no such absurdity, since he or she can separate expressiveness from the power to move. Telemann's music may indeed on many occasions be mournful, for that is a matter easily brought off by any composer who knows the craft: just pick the appropriate musical materials. But on the view I am arguing for here, it is seldom moving, even when it is mournful, because that requires not merely writing mournful music but writing *beautifully* mournful music—which, needless to say, is a very difficult thing indeed. It is, of course, what distinguishes the composer of talent (which Telemann certainly was) from the composer of genius (which he certainly was not).

Many more points might usefully be made in support and explanation of the account of musical arousal that I have tried to give. Necessity forbids them. My account, however, would be seriously flawed if I did not take at least passing notice of two very obvious objections the emotivist is likely to make straightaway. The first is the familiar charge, which I have already met and answered in other contexts, of overintellectualization of the musical experience, in this instance with the quite specific target of emotion in sight. For I have emphasized, in my Uncle Charlie explanation of how Josquin's "Ave Maria" moves me, the beliefs about the music I must entertain in order for emotional excitement to take place. Surely, though, the emotivist will reply, my head isn't filled with all that propositional baggage of polyphony, voice-leading, canon, cadences, and climaxes. If it were, such preoccupation would be utterly inimical to emotive arousal. This is *emotion* we're talking about, not cold, calculating ratiocination. The music reaches out with its soft, enveloping arms and gathers us up into its warm, emotional embrace. Feeling, not thinking, is what is going on here.

I have dealt at some length, at other places in this book, with the charge that I am imputing too much propositional knowledge and conscious ratiocination to the musical listener. And to a large extent the answer I have given in those places applies with equal force here. But as we are concerned now specifically with the emotions, it might be well to focus the argument in a slightly new way. I am saying that my beliefs about music function in the same way to account for my being moved by music as my beliefs about Uncle Charlie function to account for my being angry at him. The reply is that when moved by music I am "transported," as it were, and cannot be consciously entertaining beliefs about how the music is going: how beautiful some passage is, or how wonderfully some stretto is handled, or how smoothly a recapitulation is introduced, and so on.

My reply, to begin with, is that sometimes that is exactly what is consciously going on, when I am moved by and emote over music, just as I am often conscious, when I am angry or depressed or overjoyed, whom I am angry at and why, what I am depressed or joyous about and why. On the other hand, of course, sometimes I am in a transport of delight over a musical passage, deeply moved and but dimly (if at all) aware of what I am moved by or why. But not to worry: for neither must I be conscious at the time I am in a towering rage at the lying of Uncle Charlie of exactly what practical syllogism leads me to the point of grabbing for his throat. I am, as they say, in a blind rage. It is only afterward, in a cooler moment, that I can analyze my beliefs.

A passage from C. I. Lewis in a related vein may be helpful here. He writes, in *An Analysis of Knowledge and Valuation*:

> If in walking I turn right instead of left at a certain junction, you will attribute that motion of my body to me as my act; and so will I; though it may be that neither of us could find indication of deliberate decision or explicit prevision or any definite assessment of values in the initiation of it. If you ask me why I took this turn, I shall doubtless reply by indicating an objective which lies in this direction; "This street will take me home." I consider that the course taken was something which I did; and did for the reason assigned; even though from the time I took the turn until you made inquiry I had not thought of the matter at all. . . . I took no thought upon alternatives and made no judgment; the process might well be said to have done itself.[9]

It is the same with emotion as with action, to which it is, needless to say, intimately connected. The beliefs and intentions that make my actions intelligible, and make them my *actions*, must, of course, be available for retrospective analysis, but this in no way implies that I have consciously run over them in my mind in the heat of the moment. Likewise, surely, with the beliefs that inform my emotions: whether or not they are present to consciousness in the height of passion, they must be recoverable after the fact if we are to make sense at all of our emotional lives and understand what in fact an emotion is. Far from being inimical to emotion, belief is, in most ordinary circumstances, absolutely essential for it; and if the emotion is musical, it is about music that the belief must be. This I find altogether congenial and plausible. For music, like all of the arts, is, as I have been arguing, a thing of the intellect and

9. C. I. Lewis, *An Analysis of Knowledge and Valuation* (La Salle, Ill., 1971), p. 7.

not of the nerve endings. It is a thing of perception, of course, but one hardly needs to argue nowadays that perception too is a thing of the mind.

The second objection I want to consider is more serious, because it seems to undercut the very analysis of emotion that I have been relying on here to make out my case. I have been arguing that when I am in an emotional state, there must be an object of my emotion, and there must be some belief or set of beliefs about that object causing me to be in that emotional state vis-à-vis that object. (I am angry at Uncle Charlie because I believe he is lying about Aunt Bella.) And further, I have argued that music provides neither the objects nor, therefore, the belief-opportunities that would make it possible for musical works to arouse such emotions as anger, sadness, joy, hope, and the like. Finally, I have laid it down as a condition that if music moves us emotionally at all, it must do so in just the ordinary way that other things do: there must be objects of our emotions and beliefs about these objects. These are the presuppositions on which my whole analysis of how music moves has been based.

But, it might be argued, there are, after all, such things as objectless emotional states. Even the ordinary emotions such as sadness, hope, and the like *sometimes* (if infrequently) lack objects, at least temporarily. Who has not experienced, for example, that scourge of middle age: waking up in the middle of the night with a vague and disturbing feeling of anxiety over nothing in particular, which pretty soon finds more than enough of the usual objects to fasten upon—unpaid bills, unexplained pains, ungrateful children, unwanted troubles. But if such emotions can exist without objects, why could it not be the case that music is sad and happy and angry and so forth by being, somehow, peculiarly suited to arousing these emotions in their objectless incarnations, like my middle-of-the-night anxiety? Nor, being objectless, would they require the usual beliefs that music, clearly, is not able to provide. And why could not music be moving, then, in virtue of this: in virtue of arousing these emotions in their beliefless, objectless form?

It is just such a possibility that Peter Mew raises, arguing that "even when music expresses a core emotion [like sadness or anger] which in extra-musical contexts would necessarily take an object, it does so objectlessly." As Mew spells out the view:

> On some occasions the feeling aroused remains objectless throughout the piece; on others the feeling is aroused initially in an objectless way and then an object or collection of objects comes to mind, vaguely or clearly, continuously or discontinuously, as though the music were seeking and inducing me to seek objects appropriate to its dynamic. The important point here is that the music arouses and gives expression to an objectless emotion *before* it induces me to think of any object(s). In both cases, then, we have an instance of the arousal and expression of an objectless core emotion. Music makes, so to speak, straight for the inner life to awaken and perform an emotion thereby revising the normal extra-musical emotional process in which a person's emotion is aroused, in the first instance, by the presence, real or imaginary, of an object.[10]

I perceive (at least) three serious problems with this view, any one of which would be sufficient to make me very doubtful of its workability. Together they seem to me to make it an improbable view indeed.

To begin with, Mew gives us absolutely no clue, so far as I can make out, how music could possibly arouse objectless emotions. He says that "[m]usic makes . . . straight for the inner life to awaken . . . an emotion thereby reversing the normal extra-musical process in which a person's emotion is aroused, in the first instance, by the presence, real or imaginary, of an object." Music makes straight for the inner life: it is one of those all-too-familiar claims about the mysterious powers of music, claims we have had since Orpheus tamed the

---

10. Peter Mew, "The Expression of Emotion in Music," *British Journal of Aesthetics* 25 (1985), 34.

wild beasts. It could have come straight from E. T. A. Hoffmann or Isadore of Seville. But surely we want more than an enthusiast's assurances that music, or anything else, can entirely reverse the usual pattern of our emotional lives before we accept such an audacious claim. We want some believable account of how the thing is done. The neuroscientist can give such an account of how direct stimulation of the brain produces emotions without objects; and I dare say we are not without some reasonable idea of how and why middle-aged men wake up at night with "free-floating anxiety." Can anyone give us a really plausible explanation, not just wild speculation, of how the art of music intervenes in human physiology to cause people to become angry and sad, hopeful and happy, in the complete absence of the features of the world that these emotions are ordinarily caused by and interact with? In the absence of such an explanation, I would have to have pretty overwhelming evidence that music does indeed arouse objectless emotions before I would accept the fact, and I patiently await its as yet undreamed-of explanation.

And that leads us to the second difficulty in Mew's account. His attempt to convince us that music does indeed arouse objectless emotions is very feeble, simply without merit, and will impress only those who are already convinced. He writes: "In defense of *this* claim, it appears that I can do little more than suggest that the reader reflectively revisit his musical experiences. However, *that*, I believe, should clinch the matter."[11]

Well, surely, if our musical experience really could clinch this matter in Mew's favor, I would not be penning these dissenting remarks, and a whole host of other writers from Hanslick to the present crop of musical cognitivists would not have penned theirs. But the fact is that I do not think I feel objectless sadness, or any other kind, when I listen to the second movement of the *Eroica*; moreover, I do not perceive any evidence that others feel it either. Even objectless emo-

11. Ibid., p. 35.

tions, after all, regularly manifest themselves in behavioral responses. Nameless fear and free-floating anxiety, alas, have their way with us, as our helpmates and colleagues will attest to. I have reflectively visited and revisited my musical experiences many times and will, I hope, continue to do so with pleasure. I don't think that will help Mew's position. It surely will not *clinch* it.

Finally, let us consider the picture of the musical experience that Mew leaves us with, in talking about the cases in which, on his view, the objectless emotions that music is supposed to arouse take up appropriate objects, as objectless emotions under normal circumstances are wont to do. He writes, "although it is true that when a piece of music arouses sadness in a person it does so objectlessly, at least initially, it is also true that . . . its expressive power may induce the listener to seek for appropriate objects."[12] How should we imagine this to take place? Much, I suppose, in the way my objectless, middle-of-the-night anxiety leads me on a tour of all the unsolved problems of my life I went to bed with. God knows, there are enough things for anyone to be angry about that the angry contortions of the *Grosse fuge* will not want for objects; enough things to be miserable about that the mournful accents of Mozart's D-Minor Quartet will not fail to find reverberations in any listener's life; and so on.

But Mew's idea that the serious listener to music alone will be, as he says, induced by the music to seek objects for the objectless emotions supposedly aroused is bizarre. If, for any reason, I let myself be induced by the music to start thinking about the things and persons I am angry with, if it is angry music, or sad over, if it is sad music, I have lost concentration. If I am thinking about all of the things that make me angry, I have stopped listening to and enjoying the *Grosse fuge*; or, if I can do both at once, the former is irrelevant.

Let me suggest a completely uncontroversial way music can

12. Ibid., p. 40.

arouse the life emotions, which all of us recognize and which, it seems to me, is something like a *reductio* of the musical listener Mew envisages. It is perfectly consistent with musical cognitivism and goes something like this. The listener *recognizes* the quality of mournfulness in the second movement of the *Eroica*. This recognition reminds the listener of all the things she is unhappy about these days; and the contemplation of these things makes her unutterably sad—she cries. In this way the second movement of the *Eroica* succeeds in making the listener sad. But it is not Beethoven's success; it is the listener's failure.

No: I do not think that the existence of objectless emotions holds out any hope—if that is the right word—for musical emotivism.

I said at the outset of this chapter that the conflict between cognitivists and emotivists is an "ancient quarrel." Let me conclude it by pointing out that it is an "ancient quarrel" still enduring; that I have been beating not a dead horse but one that is alive and kicking. If that is not implicit in the discussion of Mew, then consider the following explicit example of its survival. Jerrold Levinson, a philosopher for whom I have the greatest respect, writes in a recent paper:

> Of course, the exclusively cognitive response to expression in music is a possible mode of aesthetic involvement—the detached, critical mode of the auditory connoisseur. To be sure, one can detect expression without being moved, and one can come to understand a work's moods without necessarily mirroring them. But the detached mode of involvement is just one mode among several which can be adopted, and is hardly the only aesthetically recommendable one. Its aesthetic superiority over a more open and inclusive mode of involvement—in which one both registers *and* reacts to emotion in music—is at least questionable.[13]

13. Jerrold Levinson, "Music and Negative Emotion," *Pacific Philosophical Quarterly* 63 (1982), 334–335.

Who would not agree that the cold "detached mode of involvement" is not the only mode of involvement with music or even the superior one? And who would not agree that emotional involvement with music is a very desirable thing? But the only alternative recognized here to the coldly analytic perception of music in general, and its expressive properties in particular, is once again the arousal of the emotions to which those properties correspond: love, fear, despair, anguish—the lot. And once these rules of the game are adopted, the game is already lost. For all the ingenuity in the world—and the author in question has plenty—cannot show us how music can really raise the emotions above named. He all but admits it, as others before him have done in the end, when he concludes in one place: "It is time to say clearly that the standard emotional response to a musical work, e.g., what I have called a sadness-reaction, is not in truth a case of full-fledged emotion."[14] How could he have concluded otherwise? How can music make us sad? How can sadness be the "standard emotional response" to a musical work? If a piece of music makes someone sad, or frightened, or despairing, or angry, you can be sure the reaction is either personal or pathological.

This knot cannot be untied; it must be cut. The alternatives are not being scared, saddened, sorrowed, enraged by music or being unmoved by it. That is a false dilemma. Music is sometimes moving and sometimes not; sometimes expressive and sometimes not; sometimes movingly expressive and sometimes not. It can be expressive and unmoving, inexpressive and deeply moving. And the explanation of how music stirs us is no more arcane than the explanation of why I get angry at my Uncle Charlie. The explanation, if I am right, is, indeed, so obvious and humdrum that it will doubtless be a great disappointment to many who believe in Oscar Wilde's dictum that the truth is seldom pure and never simple. Well,

14. Ibid., p. 332.

here, I urge, is the pure and simple truth about how music moves.

I have been arguing, then, in this chapter, that being moved by music and the descriptions we give of music in emotive terms—sad, hopeful, happy, angry, and the like—are independent phenomena, related only in the sense that I might be aroused to ecstasy by the beauty (say) of a particularly anguished passage in a musical work or impressed to the extent of being moved by the masterful way an aria is contrived to be expressive of an operatic character's anger or joy.

Now the function of expressive qualities such as joy and anger, in operatic music or any other music that has a text, title, or program is fairly obvious and unproblematic. The music is meant to be expressively appropriate to the plot, text, title, program, or character it accompanies. And it is these extramusical accoutrements that give the expressive qualities of the music that has them their raison d'être. We need ask no further why the aria of the Countess that opens the second act of the *Marriage of Figaro* is downcast and contemplative once we know that the Countess is in a downcast and contemplative mood and the text Da Ponte has given her expresses these sentiments.

But pure instrumental music, music alone, possesses expressive qualities as well, and very often prominently so. Some accounting for their presence is surely required. The musical emotivists have a ready explanation. For on the emotivists' view, expressive properties such as joy, anguish, hope, and the like are causal properties: causes of joy, anguish, hope in the listener. And music is moving, so the emotivists insist, just to the extent that it can arouse those emotions. To be moving, we all agree, is a nice thing for music to be. So it seems that the emotivists have a perfectly satisfactory explanation of why pure music possesses expressive properties. If it didn't, we wouldn't be moved; since composers want their music to be moving, they give it expressive properties.

But the cognitivist, it would seem, has no such ready answer to the question why music alone should possess expressive properties at all. For on the cognitivist's view, expressive properties are not causes of emotions but aural properties of the music. They play some role in making music moving, but so do lots of other musical properties. Music can be moving without them and fail to move while possessing them. So it is not clear that, on the cognitivist's view, they have any specific reason for being there at all. And that in itself might well be considered a fatal objection to musical cognitivism.

I must, therefore, turn in the next chapter to the expressive properties of music, with a view to explaining their function in the musical work. And although it will not be my contention, as it is the emotivist's, that they have in music alone a specific function peculiar to themselves, I will give an account of their functioning in musical structure that, I trust, will make their presence comprehensible, without forsaking what I take to be the palpable truth of the matter: that expressive properties are heard properties of music, not the causes in listeners of the emotive states their names describe.

CHAPTER 9 /

Hearing the Emotions)

*recognize them aurally in the music
but doesn't inherently possess them*

A ccording to the cognitivist, music possesses emotive qualities that the listener recognizes there. In other words, we hear emotions in the music, we do not feel them in ourselves. These are the qualities we are talking about when we call the music "happy" or "sad," "angry" or "melancholy," and the like.

The first question that must occur to anyone reading these words is, *How* can music possibly "possess" emotions? *How* can musical sounds be happy or melancholy or angry? People can be happy or melancholy or angry; perhaps some of the higher Primates can be, as well—maybe even dogs and dolphins. But that is because they are sentient beings. Emotions are conscious states; it seems, therefore, as absurd to impute emotions to music as to claim that a musical composition could believe that today is Wednesday or doubt that the cat is on the mat.

Many authors, including me, have offered explanations of how music might really possess emotions as perceived qualities.[1] There is not, as yet, much agreement on the question

1. For my own views on this regard, see Kivy, *The Corded Shell: Reflections of Musical Expression* (Princeton, N.J., 1980).

among those of the cognitivist persuasion. Nor, as may have been gathered from the previous chapter, is there an emerging consensus that cognitivism is correct and emotivism mistaken. There are still those who defend the view that music is sad in virtue of arousing sadness, angry in virtue of arousing anger, and so forth. What we do have, however, is a very visible group of philosophers, of varying opinions, who do not agree upon how music possesses emotive qualities but do agree that it does possess them, and that cognitivism in some form, not emotivism, provides the proper understanding of expressiveness in music.

I have had my say on the question how music embodies emotive qualities. My own view has its difficulties, as do the other contenders. And, I dare say, more work should and undoubtedly will be done on the question. But given that a substantial group of philosophers now do at least agree that cognitivism of one kind or another is correct, it is time, I think, to forge ahead and, on the assumption that cognitivism is the correct analysis of musical expressiveness, see what sense we can make of the listening experience. That is what I propose to undertake here.

To begin with, it will be desirable to know just what emotions music can possess as perceptual qualities and, if possible, why just those and not others. For it ought to be obvious that music alone cannot possess just any emotive quality at all. It hardly requires an argument that, for example, a piece of music can be mournful but not neurotically mournful over the death of a canary; fearful but not paranoiacally fearful of being kidnaped by gypsies. Music, this suggests, can possess general but not specific emotions, and in part that is true. However, it cannot be the whole truth. For, on the other hand, music can be joyful but not, I think prideful; yet here both emotions are "general," as I have not said anything with regard to pride like "that specific feeling of pride one feels at the success of one's child" rather than "that specific feeling of pride one feels after fixing a dripping faucet." It is not because pride is an emotion more specific than joy that music can be expressive of the latter and not the former. What we can say is that those emotions music is able to be expressive of it can be expressive of only in their general form. But what *are* the emotions that, in their general form, music can be expressive of?

To answer this question, let us return for a moment to the "objectless" emotions. In a seminal article on the subject, Julius Moravcsik has made an important distinction between what he calls "Platonic attitudes," such as pride or respect, and those emotions I have called, in the previous chapter, the garden-variety emotions, such as anger, joy, grief, and the like. The former require objects. One cannot, for example, wake up in the morning with an objectless, "free-floating" feeling of pride or admiration, which then fastens upon some object or other in the course of the day. Rather, "These feelings develop only as a result of our understanding presenting various objects in certain ways. Without feelings we could not admire or be proud. But without interpretations of the entities that we encounter, these feelings could not develop and have objects. These feelings develop and become directed towards objects as our understanding develops and yields interpretations of what we encounter in experience."[2]

The Platonic attitudes are, then, noncontingently attached to their objects: they cannot exist without objects, and the objects in part "define" the attitudes. On the other hand, the garden-variety emotions, fear, grief, joy, and the like, although they do not normally occur in the absence of objects, can do at times, like my middle-of-the-night anxiety, in which case they promptly take objects (except in what I suspect are pathological cases).

A recent writer on the musical emotions, Daniel A. Putman, has quite perspicaciously observed that the line between those "emotions" (broadly speaking) which can and those

2. Julius Moravcsik, "Understanding and the Emotions," *Dialectica* 36 (1982), 11–12.

which cannot be predicated of pure musical works is rather precisely drawn by Moravcsik's distinction between what he calls the Platonic attitudes and what I call the garden-variety emotions. And his explanation of why is, I immodestly assert, equally perspicacious—immodestly, because he makes use in it of my own account in *The Corded Shell*, with which he expresses substantial agreement. Putman's point is "that those same emotions that *require* objects in non-musical contexts are those which pure instrumental music cannot express. On the other hand, those emotions which are *capable* of being experienced non-musically without objects such as states of sadness or joy are those which are also the foundation of musical expression." And his explanation, which I would like to spin out and amplify somewhat with some suggestions of my own, is, briefly, "that the contour of instrumental music, with its broad yet recognizable strokes, 'fits' the contour of those broad emotions in life which, as feeling-states of the organism, can be independent of particular situations and can be transferred to a variety of diverse objects."[3] Let us see if we can understand this in terms of some nuts-and-bolts analysis.

I argued in *The Corded Shell* "that music is expressive in virtue of its resemblance to expressive human utterance and behavior."[4] The idea was that there are identifiable behavioral and linguistic routines and gestures generally associated with the garden-variety emotions, and that because we are hardwired by evolution to read ambiguous patterns as animate whenever possible—the seeing-faces-in-clouds phenomenon—we tend to "read" music emotively where it gives us the opportunity to "read" it as animate.

Now it is apparent that if this account is correct, the kinds of emotions music is ordinarily said to be expressive of—namely, the garden-variety emotions—are just the kinds we would expect to be there. What's more, the kinds of emotions it

3. Daniel A. Putman, "Why Instrumental Music Has No Shame," *British Journal of Aesthetics* 27 (1987), 57, 59.
4. Kivy, *Corded Shell*, p. 56.

seems clear that music cannot be expressive of, the Platonic attitudes, are just the kinds we would expect could not be embodied in musical compositions. For the Platonic attitudes are "intellectual" emotions, if you will, so there are no standard bodily manifestations of them. Pride is expressed by your wearing your medals, displaying your golf trophies on the mantelpiece, making your friends listen to you play the Barcarole from *Tales of Hoffmann* on the saxophone: in unnumbered and perhaps an infinite number of ways. But as there is no way for music to be perceived as being expressive of pride, in any obvious, standard way analogous to some standard mode of human behavior, that emotion is excluded from music's expressive repertoire.

Of course this is not to say there are not unnumbered, perhaps infinite, "intellectual" ways of expressing the garden-variety emotions as well. I can express my anger by throwing away my medals, locking my trophies in the closet, getting a new saxophone teacher. But the point is that the garden-variety emotions do, as the Platonic attitudes do not, have *standard* behavioral responses too. That is why we are able to ascribe them to the lower animals: we can "read" them in the visages and behavior of dogs and cats where we cannot read pride or arrogance or respect without feeling that we are overly anthropomorphizing our pets.

I have said that the distinction between what I call garden-variety emotions and what Moravcsik calls Platonic attitudes seems to demarcate rather handily the boundary between the kinds of emotions or moods music can from the kinds it cannot be expressive of: this and the distinction between emotions or moods in their general as opposed to their more specific manifestations. But let me back off just a bit. Of course the distinction is not cut sharply, with logical precision: that would be too much to expect. There are bound to be arguable cases, and it will be instructive to examine a few. My conjecture is that where the distinction between garden-variety emotions and Platonic attitudes is compromised—that is to say, where it appears that a piece of music alone is expressive of a Platonic attitude—we will find that the emotion concerned is one capable of expression in broad accent or gesture and customarily, or at least frequently, so expressed. And where the distinction between general and specific is in question, we will be up against the usual borderline cases, some of which can go either way, others of which I would reject on the basis of what my musical sensibility tells me is or is not viable as a musical interpretation (with the understanding that my taste is hardly a Kantian one, legislative for all).

Consider, then, the following three possible counterexamples.[5]

(1) Surely music can be if not prideful, then pompous. But isn't pomposity also a Platonic attitude? Surely your dog or cat cannot be pompous. That requires beliefs, attitudes, ways of living far beyond "natural expression."

(2) It is sometimes asserted that passages in Mahler's symphonies, even those having no titles or textual associations (to his songs, for example), are expressive of the "neurotic." But if music can be expressive of the neurotic, then, where it is also mournful, why not neurotically mournful? And does this not show, contrary to what I have been claiming, that music can be expressively very specific?

(3) The opening of Elgar's First Symphony is dignified and stately. And knowing something about the context in which Elgar wrote, could you not hear those opening bars, quite justifiably, in all their stateliness and dignity as expressive of the pride of an imperial race at the apex of its power? Yet pride is just one of those emotions I have identified as paradigmatic of the Platonic attitudes and, therefore, something music cannot be expressive of.

The first counterexample seems to me to be one of those cases of the exception proving the rule. Doubtless, pomposity

5. I owe the first example to Kendall Walton, the second and third to Guy Sircello.

is a Platonic attitude. But because there is associated with it a fairly recognizable, "gross" behavior pattern—pomposity struts and postures—musical gesture and tone can, in "strutting" and "posturing," come, I think, to embody pomposity as an expressive property where it cannot be expressive of the closely related attitude of pride. The case points up the fact that, although the distinction between the garden-variety emotions and the Platonic attitudes informatively draws the line between what emotions music can and cannot be expressive of, it is a rough, ragged line. But after all, the line between the garden-variety emotions and the Platonic attitudes is itself, one would think, a rough, ragged line. So although there are going to be some cases, perhaps, of Platonic attitudes being expressible in music, even though as a general rule they are not, this is no more surprising than that there are going to be some psychological states which are not going to fall *clearly* on either side of the line between garden-variety emotions and Platonic attitudes. Here, as elsewhere, we will have to be satisfied with general approximations and rough fits.

My own feeling, in regard to counterexample (2), is that had we not known that Mahler was neurotic, and an early subject of psychoanalysis, we would never have heard his music as expressive of the neurotic. Indeed, I do not think music can be expressive of the neurotic. What it can be is *symptomatic* of it. And I dare say someone who knows on independent grounds that Mahler *was* neurotic might find symptoms of neurosis in his music. Certainly what we do find in Mahler, as in Wagner, is a breakdown of harmonic "syntax" to the point where, as many have observed, atonality is the next logical step. And the cultivation on the composer's part of this syntactical breakdown may well be seen as a clinical indication of another kind of "breakdown." But I think it is both possible and important to recognize a difference between what music might be expressive of and what it might be symptomatic of. In Wagner, of course, where the text can make its contribution to our reading of the music, the neurotic may well be heard expressed in the music. In Mahler, where there is no text, the music, in my view, can only be symptomatic of the neurotic, in retrospect, as it were, with considerable help from what we know (or think we know) about the composer's psychological makeup.

The same kind of thing, I think, can be said about the opening of Elgar's First Symphony. Certainly it is dignified and stately. These are phenomenological properties I have no doubt music can have. But that the music has *anything* to do with the pride of an imperial race at the apex of its powers could, as the proposed counterexample suggests, be known only by someone acquainted with the composer and his social milieu. But as in the case of Mahler, what one would be perceiving, in my view, in perceiving Elgar's First as embodying the pride of an imperial race at the apex of its power would be something the music is a symptom of, not something it is expressive of, the difference being that whereas in the case of Mahler (if the alienist are right) we have a clinical symptom of a pathological condition, in the case of Elgar we have sociological evidence (if you will) of a political ideology and the polity in which it flourished.

It seems to me that the distinction between what music alone is expressive of and what it may be a symptom or sign of, in the composer or in his times, is an important one to maintain in principle, as difficult as it may be to make in practice. I have no wish to deny that, given what we know about Mahler's psyche and Elgar's cultural milieu, we may be justified after the fact in seeing the former's music as somehow causally connected with his neuroses, the latter's to his ideological zeitgeist. Yet it seems profoundly wrong to me to hear the neurotic in Mahler's music, or imperial pride in Elgar's, as part of the aesthetic or musical fabric. To hear, as part of one's musical experience, those things in Mahler and Elgar seems to me no more justified than Helen's seeing heroes and shipwrecks in Beethoven's Fifth: more sophisticated, perhaps, but no less an imposition upon the pure musical structure.

Thus it appears to me that, counterexamples like the above notwithstanding, Moravcsik's distinction between what he calls the Platonic attitudes and what I call the garden-variety emotions separates satisfactorily, if only roughly, the emotions music cannot from the emotions it can be expressive of; and that lends some support, anyway, to the gestural and linguistic account presented in *The Corded Shell* of how music comes to be expressive of the garden-variety emotions in the first place. But as I have said, one needn't share my view of how music is expressive of these emotions, just my belief that it is expressive of them in the sense of their being recognized in the music not aroused by it, to follow and, I hope, accept the rest of my argument in this chapter. We have some idea, in any case, of just what emotions music can be expressive of: they are not the Platonic attitudes but the garden-variety emotions in their nonspecific form. We must ask now what the role, exactly, is that they play in the pure musical experience when they are present.

Let me begin with a rather simple example: the opening measures of a movement from a trio sonata, once attributed to Bach, but now thought perhaps to be by his student Johann Theophilus Goldberg, of *Goldberg Variations* fame (see Example 12). It is the beginning of a three-voiced double fugue. The principal structural feature, to be exploited in the working out, as can be readily seen, is a contrast between two themes of musically opposite character: the one in large note values, chromatic, and descending, the other in small note values, diatonic, and ascending in contrary motion. This is the de-

Example 12. Johann Theophilus Goldberg(?), Trio Sonata in C Major for Two Violins and Continuo, BWV 1037

scription of the proceedings one musician might give to another, and it would be perfectly adequate to them. We could understand pretty much all of the most obvious aesthetic features of this movement in these terms.

But many people are quite able to appreciate this composition who are unacquainted with even these elementary musical terms. How might I explain the workings of this fugue to them? Perhaps I would suggest that they observe the contrast between the tranquil, languid theme that seems to move slowly and the vigorous, more lively theme that goes along with it and explain that it is the contrast between the languid tune and the vigorous one that is being exploited here.

And there is, of course, a third description of the proceedings I might give to the musically naive listener. I might urge that he or she observe the slightly melancholy theme that the composer combines with the more sprightly, upbeat, happy one, going on to suggest that the musical structure of the piece is built upon, plays with, these two emotively contrasted themes.

We have, then, two themes, each of which can be described in (at least) three different but related ways, calling attention to various different though, of course, related qualities. One of our themes is in whole notes, chromatic, and descending. It is tranquil, and it is a bit on the melancholy side. It is all of these things. Likewise, our other theme is in smaller note values, diatonic, ascending. It is vigorous, and it is sprightfully happy. It is all of these things. To appropriate an example of Charles Hartshorne's, from his intriguing and unduly neglected book *The Philosophy and Psychology of Sensation*, canary yellow is (of course) yellow; and it is bright; and it is cheerful; and the cheerfulness, no less than the other qualities, belongs to that color as the melancholy and happiness belong to those themes: "the emotional tonality is a part or aspect of the color or sound quality."[6]

6. Charles Hartshorne, *The Philosophy and Psychology of Sensation* (Chicago, 1934), pp. 176–177.

A further point I want to draw attention to is that the emotive qualities of these themes, in the given musical context, belong necessarily to them. That is to say, the composer could not have chosen as one of his fugue subjects that descending chromatic theme in whole notes without getting, along with it, that slightly melancholy quality, any more than an interior decorator can choose canary yellow for a room without at the same time choosing a cheerful color: it comes with the territory. But—and this is a crucial point—this choice does not mean that the composer was the least bit interested in that melancholy quality or that it plays any significant aesthetic role in his composition. Indeed, I think that in this case it does not. In this particular composition the composer, it appears to me, wanted to work out the fugal implications, the fugal permutations and the combinations, of a chromatic descending theme in whole notes against an ascending diatonic theme in contrary motion, with a more lively configuration for contrast; and he wanted to do so within the modest proportions and congenial domestic atmosphere of the trio sonata (rather than, for example, the more demanding and imposing dimensions of the organ fugue). The ascription of these goals seems all that is necessary to understand and to fully appreciate the aesthetic character of this small but well-brought-off composition.

Thus if you were to ask me what aesthetic role that melancholy quality plays in the fugue, I would reply, "None at all." If you were to ask me why, then, it is present, my answer would be that it came merely as a necessary concomitant of what is aesthetically operative, namely, the descending chromatic theme in whole notes. And if, finally, you were to press me for a method by which to tell when an expressive property is aesthetically operative in a work of pure instrumental music, I could but reply that there is no hard-and-fast rule, no formula. One does it case by case. And in the case at hand the expressive qualities do not force themselves upon us as either particularly prominent or in any need of "interpretation." I can tell you the "story" of this fugue without mentioning its expressive properties, and you will not feel the lack in the least. It is a "story" about a descending chromatic theme in whole notes and its countersubject in contrary motion. That is all. The "melancholy" and "happiness" are simply the fuzz on the peach (although helpful, perhaps, as I indicated before, in pointing out features to the musically naive.

But this does not get us out of the woods. The challenge thrown up to the cognitivist, that he or she explain the role of expressive properties in music, cannot be met by replying that they have none at all. For although it certainly is true that sometimes they don't, it seems a palpable fact of musical experience that sometimes the expressive properties of musical works are so prominent, so demanding of our attention, as to absolutely require an accounting. And were such properties extraneous to the works in which they are so prominently displayed, those works would have to be counted artistic failures for carrying such ostentatiously excessive baggage. Surely it would be too high a ransom to pay, for rescuing a theory, to have to admit that the instrumental compositions of Schumann, Schubert, and Brahms are *all* of them failed musical works, along with a large body of the classical literature up to and including Beethoven. We are obliged, therefore, to see what the cognitivist can make of expressive properties in music where they *importantly* occur.

I mentioned briefly, in the preceding chapter, the First Symphony of Brahms. I return to that wonderful work now to instance a case in point which will, I think, give us an idea how the cognitivist can explain the aesthetic role of expressive properties, when they have one in a musical composition. I might have picked any movement of this work to illustrate my point. But perhaps the most memorable—and, indeed, one of the peaks of instrumental music, both for the laity and for the expert—is the introduction and allegro that comprise the finale. And let me begin by quoting some of what that great Brahms enthusiast Eduard Hanslick had to say about the symphony, and this movement in particular, in his review of the work's Viennese première (1876). Hanslick writes:

In the first movement, the listener is held by fervent emotional expression, by Faustian conflicts, and by a contrapuntal art as rich as it is severe. The Andante softens this mood with a long-drawn-out, noble song, which experiences surprising interruptions in the course of the movement. . . . The fourth movement begins most significantly with an Adagio in C minor; from darkening clouds the song of the woodland horn rises clear and sweet above the tremelo of the violins. All hearts tremble with the fiddles in anticipation. The entrance of the Allegro with its simple, beautiful theme, reminiscent of the "Ode to Joy" in the Ninth Symphony, is overpowering as it rises onward and upward right to the end.[7]

When the reader recalls that Hanslick is famous, even infamous, for his view that expressive properties play no essential role in music, even, at least as I read him, that music is completely unable to be expressive of the garden-variety emotions, this exercise of Hanslick's in emotive music criticism amply attests to the force with which the expressive properties of Brahms's First Symphony must impress themselves upon the listener. Here is the purist, in spite of himself, practically swept away by the expressiveness of Brahms's work, "contrapuntal art as rich as it is severe" to the contrary notwithstanding. Such expressive properties surely must have a musical function, or we have here musical anatomy as superfluous as the vermiform appendix and as prominent as an elephant's proboscis. What can that function be?

The answer, it seems to me, is surprisingly simple. The function of an expressive property in a work of pure instrumental music is no different from the function of any other *musical* property of such a work—the chromaticism (say) of that fugue subject in the trio sonata. For an expressive property *is a musical* property—as Hartshorne says, "the emotional tonality is a part or aspect of the . . . sound quality"—and its function is to be musically exploited, musically developed,

7. Eduard Hanslick, *Music Criticism, 1846–99*, trans. and ed. Henry Pleasants (Baltimore, Md., 1950), p. 126.

musically played with, musically built with and built upon, along with the rest of the musical qualities it may be in company with. That is all; and that is enough. But it is not enough, of course, merely to announce this in strong language as an article of faith. So let me try to make good this claim by looking, as I said I would, at the finale of Brahms's First Symphony, which will serve as an illustrative example.

Hanslick, as we saw, describes the symphony as a kind of expressive parade, with mood following mood, and this is perhaps the commonest way of describing the standard concert repertoire to the lay audience, the stock in trade of the program annotator. Of course we *could* describe the very same sections of the music Hanslick describes here emotively, in purely musical terms: the technical terms of music theory and analysis. We might also describe them in phenomenological terms other than emotive ones. These are the same choices we faced in describing the themes in the fugue discussed previously and, indeed, the same ones we face in describing any other music in the modern Western tradition (although some music may fail to have expressive properties).

So, for example, Hanslick describes the opening Adagio of the Brahms finale as initially characterized by "darkening clouds." As it does not appear that Hanslick thinks Brahms's music is giving a weather report, I think we can take this description as a metaphor for a dark emotive tone. My own description would be anxiety (the pizzicato passages) tinged with melancholy (the opening bars), or something like that (see Example 13).

Hanslick continues, "from the darkening clouds the song of the woodland horn rises clear and sweet" (see Example 14). Again, I do not think Hanslick wants to be taken here as suggesting we attribute representational or programmatic features to the music; so we must, as before, understand his words as a metaphor of mood or emotion. It is the feeling tone of the "woodland horn" that is being alluded to: the cheerful but somewhat contemplative, perhaps even slightly reveren-

Example 13. Johannes Brahms, Symphony No. 1 in C Minor, Op. 68, Finale

Example 13. (cont.)

tial, mood that the music possesses; the kind of mood, one supposes, that natural surroundings might arouse in a nineteenth-century Romantic with somewhat pantheistic sympathies.

The section that follows is passed over by Hanslick in his description, but it is eminently worthy of notice. In contrast to the famous horn solo, we now have (in Example 15) a rather somber and serious mood introduced by the trombones, those most somber and funereal of instruments.

That the solemnity is on the religious, "churchy" side will be suggested to everyone by the hymnlike rhythm and distinctly plagal harmonies. For those who know the musical association of trombones with the archaic and religious, this mood will be even more vividly apparent. (Is it too eccentric to suggest that Brahms is contrasting two "religious" moods here: the light-hearted, optimistic mood of secular, pantheistic nature worship with the more pessimistic, darker emotions that go with the Lutheran faith?)

The horn theme returns and is musically developed with increasing pace and urgency. Finally, as Hanslick so aptly puts it, "All hearts tremble with the fiddles in anticipation" of the wonderful Allegro theme, with its mood of steadfast confidence and joy, so well-known that it is hardly necessary to quote it here.

Now I said we might describe these emotionally charged sections in pure musical terms or in phenomenological terms that avoid emotive predicates; and so we might. There is the chromaticism of the opening, the diatonic harmony of the second section, with the characteristic "horn fifths," the modal, plagal harmony of the passage for trombones, and so on. Or if you prefer a nontechnical description of the musical surface in nonexpressive terms, the first section is agitated and muddy, the second tranquil and clear, the third rather in-between, dark but not muddy, calm and stately without the agitation of the opening phrases. Nor, of course, do these barebones descriptions even begin to exhaust the possibilities.

But here the hard-nosed "purist" might well object that since there are these other, alternative ways of describing the music, there is absolutely no reason to describe it emotively. Indeed, what grounds have I for doing so? I have already admitted that, in describing the fugue by Bach (or Goldberg or whomever), there was no need to: that everything musically significant about the movement could be said in music-theoretical terms.

The answer to the purist must be that in the case of the fugue, the description in music-theoretical terms does exhaust the musically significant features, whereas in the case of the Brahms symphony it does not. It of course does not follow that because two descriptions of something are possible, one of them must be superfluous. But how do I know that the

Example 14.

Example 15.

emotive description is not superfluous for a complete accounting of the Brahms? Well, simply because the expressive properties are just too prominent to disregard. Brahms has put
neon signs around them, hung them with bells: they are as
conspicuous as the spots on a Dalmatian. And were I to offer
an interpretation of this work only in theoretical terms or even
offer both a theoretical accounting and a phenomenological
one that avoided emotive predicates, I would leave the listener
in quite justifiable puzzlement. Why this intensely melancholy
section? Why that bright happy one? Why expressive properties at all, in such obvious intensity? It can't be an accident.
How can the musical analyst leave such questions unaddressed
and still claim to have given an adequate account of Brahms's
First Symphony?

Here, however, the purist's opposite number, the wild-eyed emotivist, will jump into the fray with an equally unwelcome suggestion. Yes, of course, the emotive properties of this symphony absolutely demand recognition and explanation. And it is clear what the explanation must bè: either that these properties are there to move us or that they are there to tell us something—to tell us about emotions or about emotion-filled happenings in "life." The former claim—that the expressive properties of music are dispositional properties with the power to move us emotionally—I have already dealt with. The latter claim must now be faced. But what is there about it that carries conviction?

I suppose the argument might go something like this. When we explain what is happening in the musical work in purely music-theoretical terms, there is, of course, no need to reach outside of the music for any part of our explanation. The terms are technical, apply only to music, and serve to render understandable the workings of pure musical structure. But where emotive terms become necessary to describe what is happening in the music, they demand at the same time an extramusical accounting. We need not appeal to "life" to explain why such-and-such a harmonic progression is the way of getting from the development to the recapitulation, but we do to explain why such-and-such a deeply melancholy progression was chosen to get from one intensely joyful section to another. Why melancholy? Surely a purely musical explanation is not possible. What we need, since we are primarily using names for the conscious states of human beings, is an explanation that brings in the lives and emotions of human beings. This sequence from joy to sorrow to joy must be intended to tell us something about human joy and sorrow; or, perhaps, it represents an emotive "happening"; or it tells an emotive story. In any event, it is in some way or other "about" the emotions predicated of it.

Now perhaps there are better arguments than this one for the "aboutness" view of musical expression. And my lack of ingenuity in thinking of any may, I dare say, be laid to my obvious aversion to such views, which, as far as I can see, deny the very premise of this book: to wit, that there is pure, non-referential music and a pure musical experience of it. But however that may be, the argument before us is not a convincing one. For there is no more reason to infer that sad music must be about sadness than to infer that quiet music must be about quietness, tranquil music about tranquility, or turbulent music about turbulence. *All* of the "phenomenological" descriptions we give of music use terms that have reference to "life" as well as to music: this is not just a characteristic of the subclass of emotive descriptions. So anyone who wishes to argue that because "sad" has a reference not only to music but, far more basically, to conscious human states, it follows that sad music must be about sadness, will have to argue as well that because "tranquil" and "quiet" and "turbulent" have reference not only to music but, far more basically, to natural phenomena and human behavior, it follows that tranquil and quiet and turbulent music must be about those things: about tranquil days, quiet nights, turbulent lives. But surely that is absurd. Because music *can* be sad and joyful, tranquil and quiet, it can represent or be about sadness and joy, tranquility and quietude; but it *is* so only in certain circumstances. Those circumstances we will get to at the conclusion of this chapter. For now, we need observe only that music alone is about nothing at all, and the inference from its sadness or joy, tranquility or turbulence, to its "aboutness" a false one. A fugue may be chromatic, and tranquil, and melancholy; but it is no more, on that account, about melancholy than about tranquility and no more about tranquility than about chromaticism.

But perhaps one wants to say that music is about itself, and hence a chromatic fugue is indeed about chromaticism. Perhaps one wants to say, further, that a musical composition is just about all of its qualities. So as the fugue is not only chromatic but tranquil and melancholy, it is about tranquility and melancholy as well. And so the defender of the "aboutness" view of musical expression seems to have his desired conclusion: the music is about the emotions.

However, the emotivist indeed only *seems* to have the desired conclusion. Actually, it is but a Pyrrhic victory. For in gaining the right, in this way, to say that sad music is about sadness, he or she has paid the extravagant price of giving up any claim to the extramusical reference of "sad," which was, to start with, the whole point of the exercise. The emotivist demands an explanation that reaches beyond the pure musical parameters because, he or she claims, we can find no reason for the placement or sequence of expressive properties within the confines of music alone. But in adopting the reflexive mode of "about," the emotivist becomes committed to just such an internal explanation and that only, and has acquiesced in the view I am defending—that the expressive properties of music are purely musical properties, to be understood in a purely musical way.

Now there may be, as I noted early on, theoretical advantages in saying "the fugue is about chromaticism" rather than "the fugue is chromatic," "the fugue is about tranquility" rather than "the fugue is tranquil," "the fugue is about sadness" rather than "the fugue is sad," assuming that these are all special cases of "the fugue is about itself." And these two different ways of talking about the same thing do make a difference: a difference in the "logical" status of music or in its "metaphysical" status. What they do not make any difference at all in is its "content," if you mean by its "content" anything beyond the music itself.

So we are again arrived at the conclusion that the expressive properties of music alone are purely musical properties, understandable in purely musical terms. And why shouldn't they be? No one, as I have argued, seems compelled to seek an explanation from the "outside" for those phenomenological properties of music which are not the expressive ones. That a composer should want to combine a calm fugue subject with a

vigorous countersubject seems easily understandable on purely aesthetic grounds, on grounds at least of musical contrast if
nothing more interesting than that. Why then need we seek
any further for an explanation of why a composer wishes to
combine a joyous subject with an anguished countersubject?
Music alone is a quasi-syntactic structure of musical properties, some of which are describable in phenomenological
terms. That among the phenomenological properties are expressive ones makes this quasi-syntactic structure more interesting to human beings but not semantic in any but an
adulatory sense of "meaningful" that is unhappily misleading.

There are musical structures stuffed with expressive properties, such as Brahms's First Symphony, and musical structures
where such properties are absent or irrelevant. In the case of
the Brahms, we must seek musical understanding not in extramusical interpretations of the expressive properties but in the
work viewed as a structure of musical properties among which
are expressive ones. And there is no magic formula, no philosopher's stone, for doing so. Indeed, it is not a philosopher's
job to do it or tell others how it is done.

But there is no mystery about it either. Some expressive
properties serve to highlight musical structure, as color might
be used by the painter to emphasize contour or mass. Other
expressive properties serve as structural properties in their own
right. And an expressive property, in a work of pure instrumental music, no more needs extramusical accounting for, as I
have said, than does any other phenomenological property of
the music. Of course, a composition may possess expressive
properties for which there seem to be no real musical functions—properties that obtrude but seem to lack for a musical
reason. However, these are cases not of musical meaning but of
musical failure. We all know such musical works. They are the
ones we describe as "overblown," or "puffed up," or "emotionally insincere." These metaphors suggest, of course, emotional "content" the composer has been unable to deal with
successfully, like a poet whose verses are not up to the subject.
In that sense they are dangerous and misleading metaphors. For

there is no content at all, and the failure is a purely musical one. Grand musical gestures, whether expressive or of some other kind, demand grand musical powers. An ambitiously expressive theme demands a superior mind for its working out, as does an ambitiously chromatic one or even an ambitiously long one. And the opening theme of Brahms's First Symphony, in all of its overpowering emotive intensity, could no more be dealt with satisfactorily by (say) August Klughart (a worthy but minor contemporary) than could the chromatic subject of the *Musical Offering* be worked out to a really satisfactory conclusion by Telemann. But whereas Telemann's failure would quite naturally be seen as a musical failure, pure and simple, the failure to deal with expressive properties tends to be seen as a failure to deal with content. This is a mistake. The latter is a musical failure too, and nothing more.

Needless to say, it is no accident that expressive properties abound in musical works of the Romantic period. That fact requires an explanation, and it has one. Certainly, many Romantic composers thought they were "saying things" about emotions or about themselves when they wrote expressive music; and that is no doubt one of the reasons they did so, since they also thought it was important to "say things" in music about emotions and about themselves. But we needn't share their views or use their views to interpret their music. This was neither the first time nor the last that great art has been created under the aegis of false or even absurd theories. The important point is that those who wrote pure instrumental music in the nineteenth century were also serving another mistress: the Muse of pure musical structure, who sponsors expressive properties as well. If Brahms may have thought he was "saying things" about emotions or about himself in writing the First Symphony (and I have no idea whether he did or not), what he *did* do was write one of the most successful pieces of pure instrumental music in the repertoire. Whatever else he may have thought he had done, possible or impossible, *that* he did.

I have not, to be sure, lost sight of a point I made in passing, earlier, that because music can possess expressive properties, it is susceptible of extramusical interpretations that rely upon them. And I revert to that point in concluding this chapter.

One way of thinking about logical systems is simply as sets of rules for manipulating physical marks on paper. On this way of thinking, we are not to imagine the horseshoe symbol as meaning "therefore" or the wedge as "or." Indeed, we are not to think of these logical connectives as *meaning* anything at all. Rather, we are to represent them to ourselves merely as "objects" that the rules tell us we can put together with certain other "objects" in certain, permissible ways and not others. When we think of a logical system in this way, it is an "uninterpreted" logical system.

Of course we can, for various reasons, put an interpretation on a system if its logical structure is amenable. That is what we are doing when we say that the horseshoe means "therefore" and the wedge "or." In that case the system is no longer an uninterpreted system but an interpreted one.

Now it seems to me that an illuminating way of looking at pure instrumental music is as an uninterpreted structure. But like an uninterpreted logical system, it can be interpreted in ways that the nature of its structure permits. Because a piece of music can be calm and then agitated, it can be interpreted as representing, perhaps, a calm and then agitated life or a tranquil and then stormy seascape. And because a piece of music can be melancholy and then joyful, it can be interpreted as representing a melancholy and then joyful human experience or a melancholy followed by a joyful event. The obvious question to ask, of course, is *when*, under what conditions, are we entitled to interpret a musical structure? And the natural answer is: when the composer licenses it.

Beethoven, for example, invites us—no, demands us—to interpret the quiet ending of the *Coriolanus* Overture (Example 16) as representing the death of Coriolanus, or at least as having reference to some event in his life appropriate to the music,

Example 16. Ludwig van Beethoven, *Coriolanus* Overture, Op. 62

simply by giving that title to the work. Suppose it had had no title at all, but merely an opus number? Beethoven, being the kind of composer he was, produced, in the *Coriolanus* Overture, an aesthetically perfect piece of instrumental music that can be appreciated on its own terms. And the unusual, quiet ending, being a thematic return of the noisy opening, is perfectly justified as a rounding out of the pure musical design. But the title and Beethoven's well-known intentions in writing the work, along with considerations of pure musical design, give the close a more complete and satisfying explanation than a purely musical explanation would do. In any case, the point is that music, because it has the phenomenal properties it does, is amenable to various kinds of extramusical interpretations appropriate to them, as the horseshoe is amenable to the interpretation "therefore" because of its purely logical properties. The *Coriolanus* Overture is to Brahms's First Symphony as applied is to pure mathematics.

At this point, I imagine, someone might suggest that if any piece of "pure" instrumental music *can* be interpreted, which I freely admit, there seems to be no compelling reason why it *shouldn't* be, if a listener finds that interpretation facilitates his or her enjoyment of the work. What is wrong with Helen's hearing heroes and shipwrecks in Beethoven's Fifth if she is clever enough to do so? Indeed, shouldn't we applaud her cleverness?

Many answers might be given to this question, as I suggested early on. But, it seems to me, the most readily apparent one is that to put an interpretation on a piece of music alone is to close oneself off from one of the most satisfying and engrossing experiences the arts have to offer us. I dare say there are many people who cannot enjoy pure instrumental music without making up stories, without interpreting it, which, of course, is to say that they cannot enjoy pure instrumental music at all, since what they enjoy is not the work of pure music but another work, a work of interpreted music, which they have produced in collaboration with the composer. Perhaps pure instrumental music is caviar to the general. I guess I really think it is. But if that conclusion comes across as being intolerably elitist, let me add, in amelioration, that caviar is, after all, an *acquired* taste.

CHAPTER 10

The Profundity of Music

I have presented here a version of what I take to be musical "purism": that is to say, the doctrine, roughly speaking, that pure instrumental music, "music alone" as I have called it, is a quasi-syntactical structure of sound understandable solely in musical terms and having no semantic or representational content, no meaning, making reference to nothing beyond itself. To be sure, my "purism" differs in a crucial way from that doctrine as it is usually understood. Musical purism is customarily thought to deny emotive "significance" in any of its possible forms to music. It is customarily thought to deny that music can, as part of its aesthetic purpose, arouse or have reference to, or depict, or represent, or present, or embody . . . the garden-variety emotions. Or, to put it another way, it is customarily thought to deny that emotive descriptions of music are possible. But I, of course, believe that music does present or embody the garden-variety emotions as part of its aesthetic fabric, at least on some occasions. Nevertheless, if the core doctrine of musical "purism" is taken to be, as I think it should, that music alone is a structure without meaning or reference or representational features, then, although I take some musical features of music to be expressive ones, I think I can reasonably claim to be expounding the true spirit of purism in music.

202

But if that is what pure music is—all that it is—then there is something very puzzling about the way people sometimes describe it, something that does not seem quite to jibe with the purist's view of music alone: more specifically, with what, on the purist's view, would and would not make sense as a possible description of pure instrumental music. Here is what I have in mind.

Certain works of the instrumental repertoire are considered to be somehow "profound" musical works: Beethoven's late quartets, Bach's *Well-Tempered Clavier*, works like that. But does that belief in their profundity make sense?

The reason for the question is this. If I were to say that Goethe's *Faust* is a profound work of art where Oscar Wilde's *Importance of Being Earnest* is not, it is clear what I would mean. The former deals with deep philosophical and moral matters whereas the latter is a clever, frothy comedy of manners with no depth at all, meant to amuse and to be enjoyed. This is not to say that *The Importance of Being Earnest* is an imperfect work. Nor need I be saying, necessarily, that it is a lesser work of art. It *is*, of course. But it is possible for one work to be more profound than another yet less perfect and, perhaps, not as good. However, and this is the crucial point, we are clear that what makes one literary work more profound than another must be, at least, that is about more profound matters.

Of course, being about something profound is not, by itself, sufficient for our ascribing profundity to a literary work. For profound subjects can be botched as well as beautiful, bungled as well as splendidly brought off. So we will surely have to add that for a literary work to be profound, it must not only have a profound subject but must treat it in a way adequate to that profundity. We may say, then, that for a work to be profound it must fulfill at least three conditions: it must be able to be "about" (that is, it must possess the possibility of a subject matter); it must be about something profound (which is to say, something of abiding interest or importance to human beings); it must treat its profound subject matter in some exemplary way or other adequate to that subject matter

204 / *Music Alone*

(function, in other words, at some acceptably high aesthetic level).

That being the case, the difficulty I am having with musical profundity is obvious. Music alone isn't about anything. Hence one musical composition cannot be more profound than another in virtue of being about a more profound subject. And indeed, if being a profound work of art requires being about a profound subject, it looks as if music cannot be profound at all, and when we call Bach's *Well-Tempered Clavier* "profound" we are just talking nonsense.

Now because the version of musical purism I espouse does countenance expressive properties, there appears to be an easy way out of this dilemma. It seems plausible for me to argue that music is profound in virtue of being expressive of the darker, which is to say "serious," emotions. Thus the somber seriousness of Brahms's first and fourth symphonies warrants their being considered more profound works than (say) his two serenades for orchestra, expressive as *they* are of the lighter end of the emotive spectrum.

Perhaps there is something to this suggestion in that it may correspond to the way many laypeople perceive and talk about instrumental music. I think such people do tend to perceive and to describe music expressive of the serious emotions as deeper, more profound, than music expressive of the cheerful or frivolous ones. And I think we can easily see why this is the case. There is obviously a connection between dark emotions and profound subjects. "Serious" literature, tragedy in particular, deals with death, crime and punishment, the problem of evil, human loss, sorrow and discontent, the human condition, freedom of will, human weakness—the whole litany of human complaints. These are the subjects we find profound and difficult, and the literature that deals with them we find profound (and difficult) on that account.

But although this may be an adequate account of what music the layperson tends to perceive and describe as profound, and perhaps even productive of a sound psychological explanation of why he or she does tend to perceive music expressive of the serious emotions as more profound than music expressive of the frivolous and cheerful ones, it hardly provides a *justification* for doing so. For if, as I argue, music alone is a quasi-syntactical structure of sounds, with no sense or reference, that happens to have as some of its properties expressive ones, there seems absolutely no reason for believing that a structure with serious expressive properties is any more profound than a structure with frivolous or happy ones. Perhaps profundity arises as a result of a work's concerning, being about, serious emotions. But as, on my view, music expressive of serious emotions is not about them, that it is expressive of them is no grounds at all for ascribing profundity to it.

I have suggested that laypeople tend to ascribe profundity to music expressive of the serious emotions and that there is no real justification for so doing. A logical next step would be to inquire what kind of music the musically learned tend to describe as profound and whether their ascriptions of profundity are any more justifiable than the layperson's. I begin this inquiry with an example.

In his book on J. S. Bach, Albert Schweitzer gives the following description of the now blind composer's last days and of his last musical composition.

> He appears to have passed his last days wholly in a darkened room. When he felt death drawing nigh, he dictated to Altnikol [his son-in-law] a chorale fantasia on the melody "Wenn wir in höchsten Nöten sind," but told him to head it with the beginning of the hymn "Vor deinen Thron tret ich allhier," that is sung to the same melody. . . .
>
> In the dark chamber, with the shades of death already falling round him, the master made this work, that is unique even among his creations. The contrapuntal art that it reveals is so perfect that no description can give any idea of it. Each segment of the melody is treated in a fugue, in which the inversion of the subject figures each time as the counter-subject. Moreover the

flow of the parts is so easy that after the second line we are no longer conscious of the art, but are wholly enthralled by the spirit that finds voice in these G major harmonies. The tumult of the world no longer penetrated through the curtained windows. The harmonies of the spheres were already echoing round the dying master. So there is no sorrow in the music; the tranquil quavers move along on the other side of human passion; over the whole thing gleams the word "Transfiguration."[1]

I think it requires no argument to convince the reader that Schweitzer thought Bach's last composition "profound," although the word does not occur in the passage. And it seems obvious too that the profundity has something to do, to his mind, with the "contrapuntal art . . . so perfect that no description can give any idea of it," manifested, in particular, in the fact that we have "a fugue, in which the inversion of the subject figures each time as the counter-subject." What can we make of this?

Counterpoint itself, since time out of mind, has been associated in the thinking of musicians with the profound and the serious. And in the modern musical era, composers of instrumental music have continually turned and returned to "learned" counterpoint, always in the interest of "deepening" their style. Is the association of counterpoint with profundity merely a psychological association, like the layperson's association of profundity with the serious emotions? Or is there a real connection, as there is between profundity in literature and profound subjects? That is to say, is there some rational justification for thinking that contrapuntal music is profound in virtue of being contrapuntal? I do not mean to suggest that contrapuntal music might be the only profound music. But if we can discover just what it is about counterpoint that so frequently elicits the judgment "profound," perhaps—if indeed that judgment is rationally justified—we may be able to

1. Albert Schweitzer, *J. S. Bach*, trans. Ernest Newman (New York, 1950), 1:223–224.

generalize from that to all profound music properly so-called. Let us see, then, where this strategy may lead.

The *New Harvard Dictionary of Music* defines "counterpoint" as "[t]he combination of two or more melodic lines," and continues: "its nature is indissolubly linked to the nature of melody. A melody must have coherence; its tones follow one another in a musically sensible way, and this is true for melodies combined contrapuntally no less than for those that are not."[2] The challenge of counterpoint, therefore, is, most simply stated, to juggle successfully a complex function of two variables: the number of melodies combined together, and the intrinsic, melodic interest of each of those melodies. An additional parameter that has become inseparable from the art of counterpoint is what might be termed the principle of "melodic economy," which is to say, the use of as little melodic material as possible, commensurate with intrinsic melodic interest. This principle expresses itself in all of the familiar contrapuntal artifices that composers have indulged in throughout the centuries: combining a melody with itself (canon or imitation), combining it with itself in larger or smaller note values (augmentation and diminution), combining it with its mirror image (inversion), combining it with itself, back to front (crab). I call it the principle of melodic economy because, in all of the above-mentioned relationships, the trick is to combine a melody not with a different melody but with itself or some recognizable version thereof. This is particularly plain in the Bach chorale prelude that Schweitzer so admires for its use of the theme's inversion for the countersubject each time. And Bach's feat here is all the more remarkable, all the more difficult, because the theme he is using, that is, the chorale melody "Wenn wir in höchsten Nöten sind," preexists his use of it, thus putting an added constraint on the composer, since he is not free to invent any theme he likes that can go with its own

2. Mark De Voto, "Counterpoint," *The New Harvard Dictionary of Music*, ed. Don Randel (Cambridge, Mass., 1986), p. 205.

inversion but has to do it with a theme already given. That theme he can, indeed, meddle with to a certain extent, but not beyond the point where it would become unrecognizable.

In the modern era, in which the institution of instrumental music as we know it came into being and flourished, this juggling act has come to represent perhaps the preeminent symbol of musical craftsmanship and learning, venerable with age and almost mystical in significance for the musician. Certainly it has come to be associated with the notion of profundity. But what makes that association more than psychological or sociological? Certainly, that contrapuntal music is difficult to write and venerable with age does not alone speak for its profundity.

Let me return to Bach's last composition: the chorale prelude on "Wenn wir in höchsten Nöten sind." In it each phrase of the melody is treated as a fugue theme, with the counter-subject always an inversion of the subject. Because the chorale melody preexisted the composition of his work, it seems entirely appropriate to describe what Bach did as *discovering* that the chorale melody could be treated in this way.[3] That is to say, Bach discovered that (with suitable tinkering) each phrase of the chorale could be accompanied with its mirror inversion. The chorale was there. Bach discovered and revealed to us through his chorale prelude that it contained this "potential" (if you will) within. Bach's contrapuntal art here is the "art of the possible": an art of discovery, of revelation.

Now this, of course, is a special case. But might we not generalize from it to counterpoint as a whole? What we find so mysteriously fascinating about contrapuntal music, I want to suggest, is that it seems to us to reveal in some deep sense the very possibilities of musical sound itself. Whether we start

3. In suggesting the possibility of musical composition as discovery, I spin out a suggestion that I have made in a rather different context twice before: "Platonism in Music: A Kind of Defense," *Grazer Philosophische Studien* 19 (1983), and "Platonism in Music: Another Kind of Defense," *American Philosophical Quarterly* 24 (1987).

with preexistent material, as Bach did in his chorale prelude, or start from scratch, by devising our own fugue subject and then putting it through its paces, it is tempting to describe the process here, more perhaps than in any other kind of music, as the "discovery of possibilities." The contrapuntist seems to us as an explorer: he or she discovers what sound can do, reveals the possibilities of a theme: with what it can be combined and how. If melody appears to us as the most basic music—a melody, after all, is a complete musical composition—then counterpoint, whose "nature is indissolubly linked to the nature of melody," is the ultimate musical art, for it pursues to the outer limits the ultimate possibilities of melody, in terms of melody's possible combinations with itself. If melody is for us the simplest complete entity in the musical universe, then the contrapuntist, not the "tunesmith," is the ultimate "melodist" and, in so being, the Columbus and the Newton of our musical universe.

It appears now that we really do have a leg up on the problem of musical profundity. Recall that the first condition for a work's being "profound" is that it be able to have a subject matter, that it be able to be about something. And recall, further, that music alone, being without subject matter, being about nothing, posed a seemingly insuperable problem in that regard. But now we have found that one kind of music, contrapuntal music, seems, perhaps more frequently and consistently than any other, to be thought "profound" by the musically learned. We have found too that here we are more strongly tempted than anywhere else in music to think of composition as a discovery of possibilities and music hence to be about these possibilities, about the possibilities of musical sound or, in words we have previously used, about music itself. We have, then, a subject matter for just that kind of music which is most frequently associated in the mind of the musician with the musically profound. And the rest follows directly.

Our second condition for the profundity of a literary work

was that it be about a profound subject: a subject of abiding interest or importance to human beings. That condition can immediately be seen to be fulfilled by contrapuntal music, for it is a matter of observable fact that instrumental music is of abiding interest and importance to a significant number of human beings. And as the subject matter of counterpoint is the possibilities of musical sound—that is, music—it is a subject matter *eo ipso* of abiding interest and importance to that same significant number of human beings.

It is clear, of course, that we would not call all contrapuntal music "profound." But that coincides completely with our third condition for profundity, namely, that the profound subject matter be treated in an exemplary way, a way appropriate to the subject matter's profundity. We find Bach's counterpoint matchlessly worked out, that of his lesser contemporaries clumsily or pedantically or inadequately worked out. That is why we find Bach's works profound, his contemporaries' trivial. The subject matter of his contemporaries' fugues and canons is as profound as the subject matter of Bach's, for it is the same subject matter. But Bach was a match for it, and they were not.

To sum up, then, we find that contrapuntal music tends to be called "profound" by the musically learned and that there seems to be some rational justification for their doing so. The justification is that such music seems to fulfill the three requirements for the profundity of (for example) literary works. We are tempted to say that this music is about something, namely, the possibilities of musical sound itself; what it is about is of abiding interest and importance to many of us; and at least some of this music is matchlessly executed—executed with aesthetic distinction. The problem is that contrapuntal music is not the only kind of music the musically learned tend to call profound. And if it is the only kind of music that there *seems* to be any rational justification for calling profound, I think that would cast grave doubt on whether there is in fact any real justification for it. I myself would rather give up the notion that any music is profound than accept the notion that only contrapuntal music is. Surely I find the fugues of Bach profound, but so also Brahms's symphonies. And it would seem to me naked prejudice or dogmatism to give up the latter judgment while holding on to the former. Here I think we need to insist on all or nothing. Perhaps we can have it all.

I suggested, when I began this discussion of counterpoint, that we might find in it that which elicits the judgment of profundity; that something, moreover, might be the very thing we find profound in other kinds of music as well. I think we are now in a position to determine what that something is and to generalize it for all music within the tradition with which we are concerned.

I said that in the modern era counterpoint became the preeminent symbol of musical *craftsmanship*. That, I think, is the key. Supreme musical craftsmanship is, I believe, the common denominator between counterpoint and other instances of musical profundity. Where music is great, and where its greatness is seen as the result, *significantly*, of its consummate craftsmanship, it elicits the judgment "profound" from the musically learned.

But the crucial point is that although counterpoint may be the ultimate musical craftsmanship, perhaps the one most admired by the learned, it is not the only one. Craftsmanship is a relative notion. Every major style or idiom will have a concept of craftsmanship defined relative to it. The classical style, for example—and an important example it is—provides another preeminent symbol of musical craftsmanship. The style that came of age, many would say, in Haydn's String Quartets, Op. 33, and reached various climaxes of perfection in the mature works of Haydn, Mozart, and Beethoven, provides us with another concept of craftsmanship in music, one devolving on its notably "syntactic" character.

What justification, though, is there for attributing profundity to musical craftsmanship? Well, it is the same justification, generalized, that we have in the special case of counterpoint. Craftsmanship in music is the exploration of musical possibilities within some given set of stylistic parameters. What I am suggesting here is that if anything tempts us to refer to music as being about itself, it is musical craftsmanship in general and, in particular, counterpoint, its most prestigious special case.

But how, it is fair to ask, do we know when musical craftsmanship is to be singled out as an element in a composition important enough to warrant our calling the music profound? The most obvious answer is that when the craftsmanship obtrudes, when it presses itself forcefully enough upon our musical attention, we then are motivated and (perhaps) licensed to judge the music importantly craftsmanlike and hence profound, at least to a degree. But this obvious answer must be resisted, for the obvious reason that, at least in one sense, the obtrusion of musical craftsmanship is not only not a sign of musical profundity but, quite to the contrary, a form of musical ineptitude (at least when measured against the highest standards of musical achievement). The musical craftsmanship and learning of Mendelssohn's youthful string symphonies is truly prodigious. Their counterpoint and classical techniques of symphonic exposition and development stick out all over the place. But, to appropriate Alfred Einstein's fine phrase, these youthful works still "smell of the lamp."[4] Their craftsmanship and learning have not yet been integrated into the composer's distinctive style. The same might be said of Haydn's String Quartets, Op. 20; as marvelous and satisfying as the fugal finales are, they are not yet part of the classical style as are, for example, the fugal finales of Mozart's G-Major Quartet, K. 387, and "Jupiter" Symphony. Haydn had not yet achieved the integration and perfection of craftsmanship that Einstein called "that 'second naïveté' for which only a few masters in all the arts were pre-destined."[5] It is this same mastery of the

4. Alfred Einstein, *Mozart: His Character, His Work* (New York, 1951), p. 155.

5. Ibid., p. 156.

craft, making the difficult seem transparent, which Schweitzer recognized in Bach's last composition, when he wrote that "the flow of the parts is so easy that after the second line we are no longer conscious of the art."

Thus to a certain extent, it is just when the craftsmanship does not obtrude that we want to call the musical work profound. The craftsmanship must be there, and it must demand our attention as a primary factor in our musical experience of the work. But craftsmanship must be supremely well brought off for us to call a work possessing it profound on that account, and supremely well brought off craftsmanship is just the kind that is so well integrated into the musical work—and into the composer's personal style—that "we are no longer conscious of the art. . . ."

Nor is this inconsistent with our intuitions about the profound in the literary arts. A novelist may deal with a profound subject matter and may, indeed, have original and important things to say about it. But if the subject matter, regardless of how profound and informative it might be, fails to be treated in a novelistically successful way, fails to become "literature," we will not see the work as a profound novel, although we may see it, perhaps, as a profound contribution to its subject. The dialogues of Plato are profound literary as well as philosophical works; those of Bishop Berkeley, for all of their philosophical profundity, fail to achieve literary profundity for just the reason cited above. The characters are wooden, and the philosophy sticks out, when the works are viewed as literature.

We are now in a position to ask whether this proffered analysis of profundity in music fulfills the conditions laid down previously for success. And on first reflection it does seem to do so. The first condition, it will be recalled, is that a work be about something. In the case of profound musical works, that condition is fulfilled, in the present analysis, in that such works are profound in virtue of their consummate craftsmanship, which, we are tempted to say, makes them "about" music itself: "about" the possibilities of musical sound.

The second enabling condition for profundity is that the work be about something profound, have a profound subject matter. And as musical sound appears to be, for many people, of abiding interest and supreme importance, that condition too seems to be satisfied by at least some musical works.

Finally, we said that the subject matter of a profound work must not only be profound but be treated in a way adequate to that profundity: must be treated in some artistically supreme and exemplary way. And that condition seems, indeed, to be embodied in Einstein's requirement that supreme musical craftsmanship not "smell of the lamp" but achieve the transparency of what he calls the "second naïveté" and in Schweitzer's observation that in such supreme musical craftsmanship as Bach's "we are no longer conscious of the art."

It would *seem*, then, that we do now have adequate rational justification for the ascription of profundity to some musical works, and that justification does seem to apply just where we want it to: to just those works which, in fact, musical experts and connoisseurs tend to call "profound" or its equivalent. But I underscore "seem" because the reader is likely to detect some sleight of hand here; and I think there are at least two reasons to be somewhat uncomfortable with this rather facile exercise.

One problem rests with the second condition for profundity: that the subject matter of a profound work be a profound subject matter. For we slipped rather easily—too easily, as it turns out—from "of abiding interest and importance" to "profound." The second condition is too weak if it takes as a sufficient condition for something's being a profound subject merely that it is of very great interest, even of great concern, to a large number of people. It omits a vital normative component. For profundity to obtain, we seem to require that something be not just of great concern but *worthy* of great concern, in some suitably strong sense of "worthy" (to be discussed in a moment). I dare say far more people are vitally concerned with and interested in the subject of baseball than are in the subject of determinism and freedom of the will or the problem of evil. Yet with all due respect to the national pastime, it is a *pastime*; we would hardly take it to be a more profound subject than human freedom—or a subject with pretensions to profundity at all—just because it commands great and intense interest among us, indeed greater and more intense interest, overall, than the alternative subject.

Now I say a suitably strong sense of "worthy" because there are, it would seem, subjects of abiding interest and concern to human beings, and justifiably so, that do not merit or receive the judgment "profound." Certainly, to take an example, proper nutrition is a subject of abiding interest and concern to human beings, and surely it is worthy of such abiding interest and concern. Yet we would hardly want to say that nutrition is a profound subject matter or works about nutrition, no matter how well brought off, profound works.[6]

Why is the nature of the universe (say) a profound subject and nutrition not? Not because nutrition is of no importance to us: it *is* of importance and worthy of our concern. And not, I think, because it is of "practical" rather than "theoretical" significance. For I dare say there are environmental issues, obviously "practical," that we would surely want to call "profound." I would think those practical issues which we call profound are just those which go to the moral heart of the human condition. A life without "Nature" in something like the form we now know it in does not measure up to our moral ideal of the good life for human beings; and environmental issues addressing that concern are, therefore, "profound." A life without proper vitamin supplements is not on that account morally bankrupt, as desirable as proper nutrition might be; and if the study of nutrition goes no further—in particular,

6. I owe this objection, as well as the accompanying example, to Christopher Peacocke.

does not touch the vital center of our moral and metaphysical concerns—it surely is worthy of interest and concern but not profoundly so.

We have a pretty good idea about why such questions as freedom of the will and the problem of evil are of great concern to us. Knowing why makes clear to us why we feel justified in thinking of these as profound subjects of interest, whereas the collection and contemplation of baseball cards, no matter how intense and widespread the interest, would fail to be seen as anything but trivial pursuits. The problem is that we—at least *I*—have no clear idea at all about why serious, well-educated, adult human beings should find pure musical sound of *such* abiding interest that we are moved to call the subject "profound." And without such understanding, I cannot see that we have any real rational justification for doing so. That is to say, I cannot see that we have, to paraphrase Bentham, any reason for thinking that music is better than pushpin or more worthy of our vital and enduring interest. I believe that it is, and my belief is intense, but the strength of my belief hardly counts as an argument.

Furthermore, it is not altogether clear whether the general strategy of construing musical sound as the subject of profound musical works is free of a vicious circularity.[7] For, it might be argued, the question whether musical sound is a profound subject matter cannot be answered without first answering the question whether there are any profound musical works. If musical sound just is the class of musical works, then for it to be a profound subject matter it must, one might insist, contain at least some profound musical works. Thus there being some profound musical works would be a necessary condition for musical sounds being a profound subject matter, and the circle would be closed. There are profound musical works only if musical sound is a profound subject matter;

7. I am grateful to Christopher Peacocke and Kendall Walton for pressing me on this point.

musical sound is a profound subject matter only if there are profound musical works.

The question of circularity, then, turns on the question whether it makes sense to think of musical sound as a profound subject matter independently of its containing profound musical works. And an answer, one way or the other, seems to me to be difficult to make out. If one can prise apart the question whether musical sound is a profound subject matter from the question whether there are profound musical works, then the project of understanding profound musical works as being profound (in part) in virtue of having a profound subject matter (namely, musical sound itself), although in an unsatisfactory state, may be so merely because it is temporarily incomplete, awaiting assurance that it fulfills the strengthened normative requirement of profundity. If one cannot so prise them apart, then the project is hopelessly compromised by the fatal logical flaw of circularity.

Which of these alternatives is correct I do not presently know. But even if it is the more favorable one, I must end here on a note of mystery and puzzlement. Those of us who cultivate a taste for the instrumental music of the West seem to find certain examples of it so enormously compelling and of such enduring interest that "profound" forces itself upon us as the only (and fully) appropriate term to describe them. Yet there seems to be no rational justification for our doing so. For even if the works we describe as profound have a subject matter, and that is debatable, the only subject matter they can plausibly be thought to have, namely, musical sound itself, does not bear, at least on the face of it, any obvious mark of profundity, as do such subject matters as freedom of the will or the problem of evil, love and marriage or crime and punishment, and so forth: the subjects of "profound" literary works.

Now in saying that I have so far failed to find any rational justification for calling musical works profound, I do not want to be misunderstood as denying that I have rational grounds for thinking certain musical works great works of art. I am not using the word "profound" as synonymous with the word "great" or any other word like it. I think all but not only profound musical works are great musical works. And I think we do have rational grounds for thinking some musical works great and some greater than others. These are just the usual grounds for evaluations that abound in the music-critical literature. But I take the word "profound" as not simply a portmanteau evaluative epithet. I have taken it, when applied to music, as having the same implications as it would have when applied to literature or philosophy. In other words, I have taken it seriously. And in spite of the fact that there seems to me to be substantial agreement among enthusiasts about which musical works deserve the description "profound," I fail to see any rational justification for their deserving it. Yet, for certain works, I can find no other word as appropriate. Yes: the *Well-Tempered Clavier* and the late Beethoven quartets are great works of art. So also are Mozart's divertimenti for winds. But the former are something else, they are profound, and there's an end on it.

I find myself at present, then, unable to refrain from thinking that some musical works are profound yet unable, as well, to provide any rational grounds for my thinking it. So if you ask me, now, what my justification is for thinking the *Well-Tempered Clavier* profound, the only response that comes readily to mind is that notorious misquotation: "Play it again, Sam."

within it are the seats of profundity

mystery & awe of Langer

Works Cited

Altman, John. "Reconstructing the Evolution of the Brain in Primates through the Use of Comparative Neurophysiological and Neuroanatomical Data." *Primate Brain Evolution: Methods and Concepts.* New York and London: Plenum Press, 1982.

Aristotle. *Poetics* with the *Tractatus Coislinianus*, reconstruction of *Poetics* II, and the fragments of the *On Poets.* Translated by Richard Janko. Indianapolis: Hackett, 1987.

Barzun, Jacques. "The Meaning of Meaning in Music: Berlioz Once More." *Musical Quarterly* 66 (1980).

Berkeley, George. *Three Dialogues between Hylas and Philonous.* Indianapolis and New York: Bobbs-Merrill, 1954.

Clark, W. E. Le Gros. *The Antecedents of Man: An Introduction to the Evolution of the Primates.* Chicago: Quadrangle Books, 1960.

Cooke, Deryck. "The Unity of Beethoven's Late Quartets." *Music Review* 24 (1963).

Danto, Arthur C. *The Philosophical Disenfranchisement of Art.* New York: Columbia University Press, 1986.

———. *The Transfiguration of the Commonplace: A Philosophy of Art.* Cambridge: Harvard University Press, 1981.

Descartes, René. *Compendium of Music.* Translated by Walter Robert. Edited by Charles Kent. American Institute of Musicology, 1961.

———. *The Passions of the Soul.* Translated by Lowell Bair. In *Essential Works of Descartes.* Edited by Lowell Bair. New York: Bantam Matrix Books, 1966.

De Voto, Mark. "Counterpoint." *The New Harvard Dictionary of Music.* Edited by Don Randel. Cambridge: Harvard University Press, 1986.

Du Bos, Jean Baptiste. *Critical Reflections on Poetry, Painting and Music.* Translated by Thomas Nugent. 3 vols. London, 1748.

Einstein, Alfred. *Mozart: His Character, His Work.* New York: Oxford University Press, 1951.

Epstein, David. *Beyond Orpheus: Studies in Musical Structure.* Cambridge: MIT Press, 1970.

Flew, Antony. *God, Freedom, and Immortality.* Buffalo, N.Y.: Prometheus Books, 1984.

Gould, Stephen Jay. *Time's Arrow, Time's Cycle: Myth and Metaphor in the Discovery of Geological Time.* Cambridge: Harvard University Press, 1987.

Grover, George. *Beethoven and His Nine Symphonies.* New York: Dover, 1962.

Haggin, B. H. *The Listener's Musical Companion.* 2d ed. New York: Doubleday Anchor Books, 1959.

Hanslick, Eduard. *Music Criticism, 1846–99.* Translated and edited by Henry Pleasants. Baltimore: Penguin Books, 1950.

———. *On the Musically Beautiful.* Translated by Geoffrey Payzant. Indianapolis: Hackett, 1986.

Hartshorne, Charles. *The Philosophy and Psychology of Sensation.* Chicago: University of Chicago Press, 1934.

Hume, David. *An Inquiry Concerning Human Understanding.* In *David Hume on Human Nature and the Understanding.* Edited by Antony Flew. New York: Collier Books, 1962.

———. *A Treatise of Human Nature.* Edited by L. A. Selby-Bigge. Oxford: Clarendon Press, 1955.

Hutcheson, Francis. *Inquiry Concerning Beauty, Order, Harmony, Design.* Edited by Peter Kivy. The Hague, Martinus Nijhoff, 1973.

Kant, Immanuel. *Critique of Aesthetic Judgement.* Translated by James Creed Meredith. Oxford: Clarendon Press, 1911.

Kenny, Anthony. *Action, Emotion and Will.* London: Routledge & Kegan Paul, 1963.

Kerman, Joseph. *The Beethoven Quartets.* New York: Knopf, 1967.

Kivy, Peter. *The Corded Shell: Reflections on Musical Expression.* Princeton: Princeton University Press, 1980.

———. "Mattheson as Philosopher of Art." *Musical Quarterly* 70 (1984).

———. "Platonism in Music: A Kind of Defense." *Grazer Philosophische Studien* 19 (1983).

———. "Platonism in Music: Another Kind of Defense." *American Philosophical Quarterly* 24 (1987).

———. *Sound and Semblance: Reflections on Musical Representation.* Princeton: Princeton University Press, 1984.

Kuhns, Richard. "Music as a Representational Art." *British Journal of Aesthetics* 18 (1978).

Leibniz, Gottfried Wilhelm. " Principles of Nature and Grace." In *Philosophical Papers and Letters.* Edited and translated by Leroy E. Loemker. 2 vols. Chicago: University of Chicago Press, 1956.

Levinson, Jerrold. "Music and Negative Emotion." *Pacific Philosophical Quarterly* 63 (1982).

Levy, Janet M. "Covert and Casual Value in Recent Writings about Music." *Journal of Musicology* 5 (1987).

Lewis, C. I. *An Analysis of Knowledge and Valuation.* La Salle, Ill.: Open Court, 1971.

Lyons, William. *Emotion.* Cambridge, Cambridge University Press, 1980.

MacNabb, D. G. C. *David Hume: His Theory of Knowledge and Morality.* Hamden, Conn.: Archon Books, 1966.

Magee, Bryan. *Aspects of Wagner.* Oxford: Oxford University Press, 1988.

Marliave, Joseph de. *Beethoven's Quartets.* Translated by Hilda Andrews. New York: Dover, 1961.

Mattheson, Johann. *Der vollkommene Capellmeister.* Translated by Ernest C. Harriss. Ann Arbor, Mich.: UMI Press, 1981.

Mew, Peter. "The Expression of Emotion in Music." *British Journal of Aesthetics* 25 (1985).

Meyer, Leonard. *Emotion and Meaning in Music.* Chicago: University of Chicago Press, 1956.

Moravcsik, Julius. "Understanding and the Emotions." *Dialectica* 36 (1982).

Narmour, Eugene. *Beyond Schenkerism: The Need for Alternatives in Music Analysis.* Chicago: University of Chicago Press, 1977.

Neubauer, John. *The Emancipation of Music from Language: Departure from Mimesis in Eighteenth-Century Aesthetics.* New Haven: Yale University Press, 1986.

Niemetschek, Franz. *Life of Mozart.* Translated by Helen Mautner. London: Leonard Hyman, 1956.

Putman, Daniel A. "Why Instrumental Music Has No Shame." *British Journal of Aesthetics* 27 (1987).

Reid, Thomas. *Essays on the Intellectual Powers of Man.* In *The Philosophical Works of Thomas Reid.* Edited by Sir William Hamilton. 8th ed. 2 vols. Edinburgh: James Thin, 1895.

Reti, Rudolph. *The Thematic Process in Music.* London: Faber & Faber, 1961.

Rothgeb, John. "Thematic Content: A Schenkerian View." In *Aspects of Schenkerian Theory.* Edited by David Beach. New Haven: Yale University Press, 1983.

Rousseau, Jean-Jacques. *Essai sur l'origine des langues.* Translated by Peter le Huray and James Day. In *Music and Aesthetics in the Eighteenth and Early-Nineteenth Centuries.* Edited by Peter le Huray and James Day. Cambridge: Cambridge University Press, 1981.

Savedoff, Barbara. "Intellectual and Sensuous Pleasure." *Journal of Aesthetics and Art Criticism* 43 (1985).

Schopenhauer, Arthur. *The World as Will and Idea.* Translated by R. B. Haldane and J. Kemp. 4th ed. 3 vols. London: Kegan Paul, Trench, & Trübner, 1896.

———. *The World as Will and Representation.* Translated by E. F. J. Payne. 2 vols. Indian Hills, Colo.: Falcon's Wing Press, 1958.

Schweitzer, Albert. *J. S. Bach.* Translated by Ernest Newman. 2 vols. New York: Macmillan, 1950.

Scruton, Roger. *The Aesthetics of Architecture.* Princeton: Princeton University Press, 1980.

———. *The Aesthetic Understanding.* London: Methuen, 1983.

Searle, John. *Minds, Brains, and Science.* Cambridge: Harvard University Press, 1984.

Snow, C. P. *The Two Cultures; and A Second Look.* Cambridge: Cambridge University Press, 1983.

Tovey, Donald Francis. *Essays in Musical Analysis.* Vol. 1: *Symphonies.* London: Oxford University Press, 1935.

Wimsatt, William K., Jr., and Monroe Beardsley. "The Intentional Fallacy." In William K. Wimsatt, Jr. *The Verbal Icon.* Lexington: University of Kentucky Press, 1954.

Winn, James Anderson. *Unsuspected Eloquence: A History of the Relations between Poetry and Music.* New Haven: Yale University Press, 1981.

Index

223

Library of Congress Cataloging-in-Publication Data

Kivy, Peter.
  Music alone : philosophical reflections on the purely musical experience / Peter Kivy.
    p. cm.
  Bibliography: p.
  Includes index.
  ISBN 0–8014–2331–7
  1. Music—Philosophy and aesthetics. I. Title.
ML3845.K585 1990
780′.1—dc20   89-35570